Boys on Target

Go for it!

Bury

Boys on Target

· · · · · · · ·

Raising Boys into Men
of Courage and Compassion

Barry MacDonald

MentoringBoys.com

Mentoring Press

All inquiries should be addressed to:

Mentoring Press
A division of Sagepoint Consulting Inc.
Ocean Park Box 45053
Surrey, BC, V4A 9L1, Canada

Email: info@mentoringboys.com

ISBN 978-0-9738787-3-8

Cataloguing data available from Library Archives Canada

Dedication

- - - - - - - - -

For the many boys I have known over the years who have challenged, inspired and taught me.

Contents

• • • • • • • • •

Foreword

I have known Barry MacDonald ever since I first consulted him over a decade ago regarding my son, who was struggling in school on a number of fronts. I was so impressed with his philosophy and approach that I remember saying, "Barry, you should write a book!" And he did; in fact, this is the third book he has written about a topic so close to his heart: encouraging us parents and educators to stop labelling boys and learn to appreciate them for who they are—ways to give them ballast, encouragement, and practical strategies for their journeys into manhood.

Since my days of being a frazzled and beleaguered parent talking to Barry, I have come to know him in a professional capacity and as a friend. I have had the pleasure of helping to edit his work, and the honour of welcoming him in dynamic presentations at the university where I teach. I have seen first-hand how his writings and his public presentations to sell-out audiences inspire teachers, parents, and others in the community to reframe and refresh their perspectives on boys who struggle. It is rare for an educator who works within the system to take to the podium to challenge the status quo; even in a smaller city such as Vernon, a thousand people gathered this past year to listen to his balanced and passionate message. The power of his grass roots appeal became clear when the **Canadian Association of Principals** invited Barry to offer a keynote address at their national conference. Wherever he has taken his message, he has struck a chord with parents and teachers who are asking administrators to pay attention and revisit old assumptions; his practical wisdom suggests how we can learn to see boys not as an objectified *problem* but as whole persons with strengths we can help them to uncover.

As a friend, I have had many conversations with Barry about his work with boys in schools and families, and can testify personally to his commitment and integrity. Barry's passion for mentoring boys is informed by his own childhood experiences of being raised by a single mother, with an absence where his father might have been. I have heard him tell compelling stories, full of pathos and humour, seeded with optimism—but never naive. As a professional who has consulted with administrators, school boards, teachers, parents—and, of course, boys themselves—Barry speaks and writes from a unique vantage point. He can see the forest as well as the trees—that is, the individual boy, and the larger cultural context.

Through his website on *Mentoring Boys for Success* and his newsletter, Barry has received hundreds of emails from parents and teachers about questions that keep them awake at night. He has selected several related to boys' identities, various modes of expression, and learning at home and in school. They are reprinted here. Barry has also provided fresh new commentary and revisions, since his ideas are constantly being tested in the field, and he practises the kind of creative flexibility and open-mindedness he promotes.

Whether you are a parent or teacher or an adult involved with mentoring boys in some other capacity, you will find the thoughtful, in-depth discussions in this book enlightening and deeply nourishing.

Dr. Sue Ann Cairns

Kwantlen Polytechnic University

Co-author—Strategies for Successful Writing

Preface

· · · · · · · · · ·

What You Can Expect From Reading This Book

MAYBE you have a capable and smart son who sparks with enthusiasm and drive to pursue his projects at home, but struggles with motivation to learn at school. Or maybe your son has been making the grade, but you have recently noticed his growing dissatisfaction with schooling, and you worry about his future. Perhaps you are an educator who wants to make learning more relevant, more responsive, and more meaningful for boys while also respecting the needs of girls.

It is only fair to let you know from the get-go that if you simply want to place blame or read about someone criticizing or grumbling about boys and schooling, this book is probably not for you. Twenty-five years of experience in public education has taught me that complaining without conciliation does not lead to creative and productive action. My goal is to explore how we might come together to respond creatively to boys' differing needs. I envision people taking a step back, looking at what is often defined as a problem from a fresh angle. How can we cultivate the habit of looking for strengths to tap into, rather than labels to apply or ready-made scripts to follow? If we expect boys to grow into men of character who will make a positive difference in the lives of those around them, we need to first make a difference in their lives—especially when they are floundering.

While there are many first-rate books about boy troubles that have been published over the past couple decades, *Boys on Target* offers something different.

Boys on Target reaches beyond merely illuminating the plight of boys; it provides solutions, and new ways of thinking about questions that most plague parents and teachers. Written out of my experience as educator, counsellor, and passionate advocate for boys throughout Canada and elsewhere, *Boys on Target* explores how we might collaborate creatively to respond to boys' differing needs, and what we have defined as problems.

Boys on Target also includes the voices of those caring adults who deeply desire to help boys get on track and develop their potentialities. Wherever possible, I have also tried to include some of the stories about what boys say behind closed doors in my home office or a principal's office to me about us adults—their perceptions, their worries, and their struggles. During countless interviews with boys who are fed up and discouraged with the pressures of schooling and growing up male, their stories can help us to get inside a boy's world to better understand his journey through the corridors of boyhood.

For boys to be successful, they need to be part of something bigger than they are. They need help in recognizing their gifts and limitations. They need guidance through the trials and tribulations of life. They need discipline from parents and teachers that is firm yet kind, along with the strong presence of love.

After much consideration about how to lay out the information in this book so it will be useful to you, I have chosen to handpick my newsletter articles that have received the most positive or provocative feedback. I have revised and organized them so that they can provide you with a wide-ranging overview to the many questions parents and teachers ask about boys. Each topic begins with a parent or teacher inquiry and follows with a balanced discussion and useful ideas to help you get going with helping boys. I have changed names and identifying characteristics of each inquiry without altering the meaning and significance of their accounts.

Ultimately, it is my hope that *Boys on Target* will get you thinking optimistically about boys while you also get practical guidance about common questions about boys' struggles, propensities, and potentials.

Above all, it is my belief that we can, by working together in mindful and respectful ways, make positive differences for the next generation—males and females.

The Plight of Boys

• • • • • • • • •

In many families and communities, boys' behaviour and underachievement are charged topics—contentious, complex and confounding. As the founder of a website that responds to the divergent needs of boys, author of *Boy Smarts: Mentoring Boys for Success at School*, and as an international public speaker on boys' issues, I have received thousands of inquiries from parents and teachers about boy troubles. As I travel the country speaking to educators at professional development conferences, I have discovered that scores of teachers, administrators, support staff, and school trustees are also distressed about the widening gender achievement gap.

While many once assumed simply that boys will grow out of whatever problems that are manifesting at the moment, many parents and teachers now recognize many ways that boys are at greater risk than girls for an array of problems. U.S. statistics report:

- for every 100 girls who repeat kindergarten, 194 boys repeat kindergarten

- for every 100 girls expelled from public elementary and secondary schools, 335 boys are expelled

- for every 100 girls diagnosed with a learning disability, 276 boys are diagnosed with a learning disability

- for every 100 twelfth Grade girls who carried a weapon on school property, 287 boys carry a weapon

- for every 100 girls ages 15 to 17 in correctional facilities, there are 837 boys behind bars

While researchers have long known that income and ethnicity have been shown to be the greatest predictors of academic success, increasingly they are focussing on the reality that gender is another important determinant. Simply being male puts a boy at greater academic risk, and has tremendous impact on a boy's growing personality, skills, hobbies, health, career, and his future relationships.

Even before being born, the male fetus is at greater risk of death or damage from almost all the obstetric catastrophes that can happen before birth; prenatal brain damage, cerebral palsy, congenital deformities of the genitalia and limbs, premature birth, and stillbirth are each more common among boys than girls.

By the time a boy is born, he is on average developmentally some weeks behind his sister: A newborn girl is the physiological equivalent of a four to six week old boy.

From these early months and years boys are much more vulnerable to a great variety of problems: they mature more slowly, get sick more often, and are less likely to have mastered the language, self-control, and fine motor skills necessary for a successful start in school.

Boys are at greater risk than girls for most of the major learning and developmental disorders—as much as four times more likely to suffer from autism, attention deficit disorder, and dyslexia.

Boys make up two-thirds of students in special education—including eighty percent of those diagnosed with emotional disturbances.

Boys are seventy-five percent more likely to die in accidents and more than twice as likely to be victims of violent crime.

Increasingly, we are grasping that boys have unique challenges. The 2007 **Canadian Council on Learning** report, *State of Learning in Canada: No Time for Complacency,* states that "The difference in the reading levels was more significant, with girls scoring an average of 32 points higher than boys," and that "males have a higher rate of language and learning difficulties." Educators understand that in order to become participatory citizens who can contribute to society, boys must develop literacy skills. Low levels of literacy contribute to increased chances of incarceration, compromised health, and often a sense of lifelong inadequacies. Teachers are troubled that significantly more boys than girls declare themselves to be non-readers, and that dropout rates are higher for boys than for girls—2 out of 3 dropouts are likely to be male.

When we read these worrying statistics, we may question our leadership, and wonder if we are even up to the task of parenting or educating boys.

We may look for targets to blame: the effects of divorce, lax parenting, exposure to electronic video games; some even look at feminism or the so-called male backlash.

When alarm bells are rung, some repeat the soothing mantra: *boys will be boys*. I hear others say things such as "Boys need stronger discipline" or "It's only natural for boys to dislike school. Isn't school a girl's thing?".

Most people, however, are not willing to settle for clichés or easy answers. In their desire to help boys get back on track, to become more engaged in their learning, and to develop the skills they need to make a positive difference in the world, these caring adults want more.

While many of us have common concerns, most parents and teachers understand that each situation should be viewed case-by-case, boy-by-boy. They don't want to stereotype boys, and they certainly don't want to pit the needs of boys against those of girls. Many specify that they want to avoid exaggerating gender differences and gender expectations that can lead boys themselves to believe limiting stereotypes about masculinity. Thoughtful parents and teachers want to approach parenting and schooling in ways that reflect our awareness of the different needs, strengths, and potentialities of the young people in our care.

GENDER IDENTITIES & CULTURAL EXPECTATIONS

· · · · · · · · · ·

HOWEVER different our philosophies may appear, most people who work with young people recognize that gender is one of the great organizing principles in child development.

Sometimes the terms *gender* and *sex* are used interchangeably, but the scientific view is that *sex* and *gender* are different. Sex, which includes physical attributes such as sex chromosomes, hormones, and genitalia, is biologically determined. At birth, sex is used to identify individuals as male or female.

It then becomes common that this binary division for identifying sex carries over into how we conceptualize gender. We may assume that boys behave in distinctive ways, and that girls behave in another way. Yet, we know that gender is far more complicated.

Genes and hormones do contribute to some of the different tendencies we observe in boys and girls, but these are only the beginning. Gendered expectations are taught from the moment we are born, sometimes even earlier. One study showed that parents talk more to a female fetus, use more nicknames and baby talk, and touch the mother's belly more often. When children are born, we dress baby girls up with pink bows and ruffles, while boys wear clothes that feature sports logos, alligators, and sturdy trucks. Most things in society are assigned a gender—clothes, toys, many behaviours—and even some subjects in school.

It is difficult for a child to grow to adulthood without experiencing some form of gender bias or stereotyping, whether it be the expectation that boys are better than girls at math or the idea that females are more nurturing; in the classic story of *Peter Pan*, Wendy, like her mother, loves to sew and tell stories to children, but Peter and the boys love to have adventures.

Is it true that *real boys* are born to be rambunctious, adventurous, and curious? If we expect boys will climb trees, build forts, and play tackle football, what happens when a boy is not interested in these pursuits? Is a timid and sensitive boy somehow less a *real boy* than a boy who is physically outgoing and daring? How do we regard boys who are exceptionally rambunctious, impulsive—even aggressive?

Many people worry about the emotional and psychological costs of gender stereotyping over a lifetime. From a very early age boys are encouraged to disregard their internal emotional world in order to conform to conventional notions of tough masculinity. Since a nebulous concept such as masculinity can never be taken for granted, these boys may later feel great pressure to achieve status in order to prove, over and over again, that they are *real men.*

One Size Does Not Fit All

People sometimes assume that I must hold a single view of what it means to be a boy, and a single remedy for their struggles.

While it is true that certain tendencies do exist among boys, and it is possible that some differences even appear to be genetically driven, we need to avoid the temptation to typecast and pigeonhole boys. I do not imagine there is a single cause of boys' struggles, nor do I believe there is a single remedy—certainly not *Zero Tolerance*, single-gender schooling, or a return to the nineteenth century!

Wherever boys are located along the gender continuum—from the quiet boy who is more inward and reflective—to the boy who is a regular visitor to the principal's office—we need to consider the specific needs of specific boys.

In *Boy Smarts: Mentoring Boys for Success at School*, I say: "The binary gender construct, where the world is sharply divided between boys and girls, men and women, limits our understanding of people. Some boys are more aggressive and demanding like *Rambo* while others are more sensitive. In reality, gender exists along a continuum from extremely feminine at one end and extremely masculine at the other with many types of shading of gendered states in between."

If, however, your boy is both highly rambunctious and highly sensitive, you may wonder where he fits on this gender continuum. After much observation and reflection, I have concluded that boys are better served if my earlier notion of the gender continuum expands to become more multidimensional. Expanding the gender continuum into a matrix lets us see clearly that while some boys might be positioned in the middle of each continuum, they may also exhibit, say, the sensitivity of *Spiderman* as well as the physical aggressiveness of *Rambo.*

To better understand the gender matrix, consider the characteristics of your own son or a boy you know and locate where he typically fits on the spectrum between each extreme descriptor below. Notice whether the boy you are considering primarily has *Rambo Senses, Spiderman Senses*, or something in between. After you have completed each of the fifteen dimensions, consider the whole picture, and view these dimensions as a matrix. What patterns do you notice?

Gender Matrix

Rambo Senses	Spiderman Senses
• in perpetual motion	• is calmer, sits still for lengthy period
• does not startle easily	• tends to startle easily
• sleep comes easily at the end of the day	• hard to get to sleep after an exciting day
• doesn't notice clothing or body discomforts	• complains about uncomfortable clothing
• does not notice the distress of others	• tends to notice the distress of others
• not cautious before climbing high	• cautious before climbing high
• high pain threshold	• very sensitive to pain

Rambo Senses	Spiderman Senses
• doesn't read body language well	• reads subtle body language cues
• not affected by noisy classrooms	• is bothered by noisy classrooms
• tends to prefer team sports	• tends to prefer individual sports
• prefers action	• prefers relationships
• play is highly competitive	• play is highly cooperative
• not a perfectionist	• perfectionistic
• prefers correction that is firm	• prefers gentle correction, or hints
• tendency to not pick up on social cues	• can be over-stimulated with social cues

In a culture with more flexible ideas about gender, we could easily move back and forth, and up and down throughout this matrix.

From this perspective, schools would then be challenged to provide learning activities that appeal to boys who may be all over the gender matrix. Boys who want to become hockey stars may also have a deep love of reading. Boys who seek thrills and physical challenges may also be attentive to subtle nonverbal social cues.

Rather than automatically assuming that all boys benefit from more rough-and-tumble activities, we could provide a range of activities for boys that meet varied needs—for reflection as well as for rambunctious play. We would appreciate that while many boys need recess and opportunities to get their wiggles out, others need space for quieter activities such as chess, model building, and reading clubs.

We know from nature that diversity makes the species stronger. Appreciating the diversity of all children—boys and girls—we must work toward providing a range of opportunities for learning—in realms that include the physical and emotional; technological and creative; academic and practical.

The following emails from parents about boys' diverse needs and temperaments, along with my responses, show clearly why one size does not fit all.

1   The Uniqueness of Boys

RATHER than judging children for not fitting a cultural norm, we can cultivate appreciation for their special qualities as potential resources. Consider for a moment: What if your boy is more sensitive than tough?

Boys Who Have Spiderman Senses Are Sensitive and Attentive to Their Environment

Dear Barry,

My boy is mostly shy in social circumstances and avoids sport activities. He's in Grade 4 and gets teased by the boys for being smart. He is bright, loves classroom learning, is nuts about reading and is highly verbal. In fact he started talking with reasonable clarity before he turned one year old, has great eye contact, and notices everything around him. The school is very good about ensuring that no bullying occurs and is just super about playground supervision and providing lots of activities to channel the rambunctious boys, but he's so sensitive that he notices even the tiniest of slights and focuses on them as though they were a big deal. He's overly sensitive about a lot of things and he typically cries when I try to discuss things with him. My husband says we need to toughen him up if he is going to make it in this world. He wants to put him in a sport that will teach him to be more masculine. I know that would be a disaster for my son. What do you suggest?

Jane

Dear Jane,

Putting your son in a team sport will broaden his cultural experiences only if he desires to participate. Forcing him would weaken your bond with him, and could even become a shaming experience. Perhaps your husband fears that he will have a hard time growing up if he is so sensitive. However, his desire to toughen him up so he becomes more masculine is misguided.

To begin, I would encourage you both to consider Guideline 20 in *Boy Smarts—Teach Healthy Masculinity*—which offers a list of masculinity traits that have been proven as the basis for male strength that is caring, courageous and ethical, rather than manipulative, dominating, and controlling. Your son appears to have some of the classic symptoms of a unique aspect of masculinity—*SPIDERMAN SENSES*.

Spiderman's predominant skill as a superhero is his ability to tune into his environment and perceive subtle modulations in that environment. While many boys who are oblivious to environmental and social cues struggle to read non-verbal communication and take longer to understand social mores, your son is well attuned to his environment. However, while *Spiderman*—a mature figure—manages his *Spidermantingles* well, your son is still young, and may easily become entangled in the abundance of cues and conflicting environmental messages he takes in.

You can't medically remove *Spiderman Senses*. I suspect that your son was calmer in the womb than many males, and likely had higher serotonin levels. Once born, it is predictable that he had the ability to gaze for longer periods of time than typical male babies, and was also able to distinguish another baby's cry from background noise. He most likely was also able to recognize faces of people in photographs. As he got older, I imagine that he continued to attend to people and his surroundings in a way that made people remark on his pleasant and polite manner. While most boys achieve speech clarity at age 4.5, your son began talking early and likely achieved speech clarity by age 2 or 2.5 years. At the same time as boys in kindergarten were building tall structures and knocking them down, your son probably shared his blocks, collaborating with others in building projects—perhaps with other boys with *Spiderman Senses* or girls who also were sensitive.

These emotional and interpersonal skills are highly desirable in the adult world, but because he is more sensitive than many boys, he may feel at odds with other boys at times—and they with him. Remember that children proceed with development at their own rate. While he stands awaiting an invitation to play, other Grade 2 boys may have barged in past him and grabbed the toy he wanted to play with. Misinterpreting their behaviour, he may have complained later: "No one likes me."

The best gift you can give your son is to accept him where he is, and develop an appreciation for his *Spiderman Senses.* This may involve simply understanding the *Boy-Code*, which requires boys to appear brave, show little emotion, not to tattletale, and never to cry. You might practise reframing your perspective of his *Spiderman Senses* in a positive way.

In my many years of consulting with parents about mentoring boys, I have observed that boys thrive when they feel understood and appreciated for who they are. As a boy who relaxes into his *Spiderman Senses* becomes more self-aware and self-accepting, he will also develop practical coping skills to deal with others' aggression.

When I talk with boys who are sensitive, they tell me that adults provide a haven of support and understanding. While others might tease them for being different, mature adults can reassure him that he is appreciated for his unique qualities.

Ways to Support a Sensitive Boy & Maintain Positive Connection

Listen to him—Give him the attention you would give a valued friend. Show respect for his ideas and conjectures about life. Remember that he could have limited opportunities to express these viewpoints at school, so your attentive listening really counts.

Support his preferences—Ensure that he pursues things that interest him. Leave your worries and judgments behind. Show faith in his choices.

Teach him how to respond to bullying behaviour—Take time to role-play and rehearse different responses to anti-social behaviour.

Support social activity that he is comfortable with—Consider a church youth group, a family or summer camp that emphasizes interests that might appeal to him: music, drama, computers, etc. Encourage and help arrange weekend activities with other like-minded children; these can be something for him to look forward to if he finds himself too much alone during the week at school.

Be in regular contact with the teacher—The teacher might be able to tell you about his stress level at school, especially during playtime. Also, check whether the school supports activities for boys who are sensitive. Chess, robotics, music, dance, and drawing might interest these boys more than sports.

Show faith in him—Feeling sorry for him will not help his confidence or his abilities to manage. Acknowledge the difficulties he is having, but remind him that he has managed in the past, and you are confident he can use his *Spiderman Senses* to manage this new situation.

As you help your son develop appreciation for the ways that his *Spiderman Senses* can guide him, over time he will learn not to be overwhelmed by them, but to use them well. As an adult, he will be able to use his caring and special sensitivities in a career that others will greatly respect.

2   Why is My Boy So Rambunctious?

RAMBUNCTIOUS play is not the same as violence or bullying. Guideline 15—*Avoid Reacting to Playground Rumble*—in *Boy Smarts* encourages us to become more responsive to boys' developmental needs and provide opportunities for boys to express varied needs, including the need for physical movement.

Rambunctious Play: The Trademark of Active Boy

Dear Barry,

My boy is in Grade 3 and recently got in trouble for play fighting at recess. I had hoped that he would grow out of rough play last summer but find that he, his friends, and his younger brother still engage in a lot of aggressive play. Mostly, it seems all right, but every now and then one of the boys crosses the line and someone gets hurt. Usually I can see it coming.

Don't get me wrong—they are caring and smart boys, but the playground supervisor says that there is no rough play allowed whatsoever. As a parent, I feel stuck between being my son's advocate and supporting school staff in their educational role. My son is a great kid, with a very social and wonderful personality that I do not want to alter or squash. Any ideas?

Gurmeet

Dear Gurmeet,

While boisterous active play—chasing, yelling, and charging around—is common among children, rough and aggressive play is widespread among many boys well into their teen years. Although you likely don't want your son or any of the other children to get hurt, it would be wise to consider the legitimate role that rough-and-tumble play has in his world.

You will be hard-pressed to find a pediatrician or child development specialist who will disagree with the notion that rambunctious play actually helps children—boys in particular—to develop. They will tell you that spontaneous play fighting can help boys learn to control their emotions, bodies, expression and anger; as well as to acquire problem solving, negotiating, and other social skills. They learn their own limits and those of others so that they don't lose control and hurt themselves or others. Allowing children time and space where they can just let rip is crucial—especially after they have been sitting and concentrating at a desk.

As long as no one is getting hurt, observe and supervise boys' energetic play, and intervene when appropriate. Of course it is to be expected that boys will cross the line of decorum at times, but with appropriate supervision, parents and teachers can intervene and utilize these moments to teach constructive behaviour.

I have also found that it is typical for boys to connect socially with other boys within the conventions and constraints of the *Boy-Code* that emphasizes toughness—and not crying. This code prevents boys from open displays of affection, so that teasing and rough physical play may become a way of bonding. Perhaps this roughness is not the ideal way of relating, but we must not read it as the certain sign of a troubled boy either.

Whereas girls tend to set limits with other girls through social exclusion, there is ample evidence to indicate that boys draw lines in the sand nonverbally through aggressive behaviour that is not intended to harm. For girls the conflict can span several days, while for boys the conflict is more commonly a momentary flair.

Certainly codes of safety around playground behaviour are necessary, but many parents and teachers have indicated to me that school regulations of recent years that are too inflexible can typically constrict and oppose non-threatening playground behaviour. A *Zero Tolerance* fighting policy means that boys who are very energetic during their recess break and participate in ritualistic play fighting, along with pushing and shoving, are often reprimanded or disciplined. But should *Zero Tolerance* toward violence and harassment apply to rough–and–tumble behaviour on the playground?

Wouldn't children be better served if we considered when is rambunctious play acceptable and when is it inappropriate? Perhaps a group of concerned individuals from your **Parent Advisory Council** could meet with school staff and consider how your school community could provide playground opportunities for boys—and girls—to express themselves through vigourous play that is varied and safe. Rather than banning certain playground behaviours such as tag, physical touching, and snowball throwing, the parents and school staff might reflect on more imaginative and effective ways to structure playtime while also providing some scope for energetic play.

Rather than simply outlaw snowball throwing or banning tag, for example, adults can help most by providing rules, supervising play, and teaching children how to throw snow in a manner that keeps everyone safe. Besides, providing a safe space for energetic, lively play could just help you get some peace and quiet later on!

3   How Can I Stop My Young Son from Hitting?

IT is vital to appreciate the developmental stages that children go through; otherwise we run the risk of labelling the boy as the problem. This chapter explores hitting among young boys, a behaviour common to many young children as a signal of a boy's developing sense of self and personal ownership in the world.

Hitting May be a Way that Young Boys Communicate Strong Feelings

Dear Barry,

Jacob, my 3 year old hits other children when we take him to the play area! Even if he's not playing with a toy, he'll grab it first if he sees that another child wants it and then he hits the other kid. We've told Jacob that he needs to share, and we've told him to use gentle touches, but he still hits. Does this mean he is more at the Rambo end of masculinity? Would hitting him back help him to realize that hitting hurts and that he should stop it?

Sylvia

Dear Sylvia,

It is developmentally typical for your son to hit at this age, just as it is typical of boys at age 4 or 5—and older!—to experience difficulty sitting in a restaurant. Jacob is at the *everything is mine* stage of development where children need to learn about ownership before they learn to share.

If children play together at all, it is usually side-by-side in parallel play; social interaction can often lead to conflict as children fight over ownership of toys. Because Jacob isn't old enough to understand the concept of sharing, and because he is, at his stage of development, experiencing a need to assert himself within his environment, he will act out his needs. Especially as boys his age typically have limited vocabulary, aggressive acts can be the only way boys can communicate strong feelings.

Jacob may lean toward the *Rambo* end of the masculinity continuum, and may need increased opportunities to get the wiggles out in order to engage more fully at school. However, rather than labelling him in some way, I would encourage you to view his behaviour as normal for his age and stage of development.

Of course, this doesn't mean that you let him hit other kids. So what do you do? How you structure the playtime environment is important. With shorter play periods, ensuring that he not tired or cranky when he meets with other children, remaining close by and observing his play, you will often be able to intervene before Jacob lashes out at another child. If you see him headed toward conflict, you can distract him by engaging with him in his play and letting him take the lead. If he does hit someone or act out aggressively, it is important to remain calm, not make big deal out of it, and remove him from the situation. Try again later as he needs opportunity to move through this stage and as his cognitive abilities mature, he will develop more socially acceptable behaviour.

Hitting Jacob back would only teach him that larger people can hit smaller people. Hitting children teaches them to fear you rather than trust you. It creates anger and resentment and models that violence is an acceptable solution to conflict—the opposite of what you want Jacob to learn.

An understanding of child development, along with your calm response and loving guidance, will gradually teach Jacob about turn-taking, sharing, and managing conflicts and emotions. For now, structure, prevention, calm listening, and compassion are your best tools.

BOYS IN THE FAMILY MATRIX

• • • • • • • • •

LIKE all of us, boys learn by copying. They absorb attitudes and emotions and patterns of behaviour which they see in the family and culture even before they go to school. As they get older, boys' personalities and character are influenced by many factors: the individual temperament of the boy; the family and home; the peers they encounter; and, of course, the school and the broader culture.

The first, and often most effective teachers are a boy's parents and guardians. It is not, of course, simply what parents say which influences a boy, but more importantly, how a parent responds.

Parents Want Help to Strengthen their Parenting

Knowing that children grow into the family life around them, and that over time, we become our habits, parents want answers to the questions that trouble them on the home front:

How can parents initiate meaningful conversation with boys?

How can parents foster more peace among siblings?

How can parents manage boys' rough-and-tumble play fighting? Is it even something that needs to be managed—or can it be appreciated for the ways it may improve physical strength, vent high energy, and teach appropriate social boundaries?

How can fathers forge meaningful connections with their sons, especially when they haven't had good models of fathering themselves?

How can parents cultivate compassion and empathy in boys?

How can parents respond to boys' tears of frustration in ways that encourage a healthy emotional life?

4   Initiating Conversation with Boys

WHEN boys are flooded with anxiety and anger, they may find a degree of healing simply by being listened to, attended to, and appreciated.

But what if your boy doesn't provide you with the opportunity to listen?

What if you know that he is troubled, but he sits in stony silence? How do you initiate conversation? How do you listen to his deeper self when he is locked in a silent turbulent world?

How do we listen when there are no words?

Dear Barry,

Your January article about boys and anxiety did a great job of describing the potential causes, outward appearances, and cultural factors contributing to anxiety and resulting anger. Now, I'm interested to know more about practical ways to engage my 10 year old son in talking about his chaotic inner world. When I try to start a conversation, he usually stares off into the distance, shrugs his shoulders, or mutters, "Whatever."

What are good openers to get us started? You see, I understand the problem but I get stuck with my response. Some examples of how to go about it exactly and to make conversation flow better would be helpful.

Dr. SuLyn

Dear Dr. SuLyn,

You are wise to be concerned about how conversation flows between you and your son when you have reason to believe that he may be stuck in an emotional spin cycle. Boys often can mask their strong emotions with a show of indifference or bravado that makes them hard to reach.

While I'd like to offer some ideas on how to initiate and strengthen conversations with your son, I first need to stress that encouraging boys to open up is less about getting them to talk, and more about attending to them in a way that lets them feel heard, whatever they say or don't say.

Children learn about themselves by the way we communicate with them— particularly when they are agitated.

Instead of listening—really listening—it's all too common to focus on what we're planning to say in response, or how we might direct conversation.

Instead of really listening, we might intellectualize or analyse what our child is saying: "Sounds like you have a case of the pre-game jitters to me."

Instead of really listening, we might cut off a child's rambling story to lecture or preach—or even interrogate: "What did you do to make him so angry?"

Instead of really listening, we might leap straight into advice: "You need to stand up for yourself…"

We might even interrupt our children mid-sentence, often in an attempt to relieve our own anxiety rather than providing a safe place for children to express theirs.

And we might go elsewhere in our minds rather than being present for our children.

Boys themselves sense when we are worried and distracted. When they observe us pushing away our own anxieties, perhaps taking refuge in gossip or in chatter about mundane details, they may learn to discount their inner worlds. When boys see us try to numb our own emotions of fear, sadness, and anger, maybe even by using substances—they may conclude that vulnerable feelings should be dulled, deflected, or hidden.

In our own parenting, it's hard not to repeat patterns and habits we learned in our own childhood. Our childhood experiences of being loved find expression in our capacity to love our children later on. Our unhappy experiences—perhaps of being criticized, ignored, or yelled at—often get re-played when we are parents.

More important than any conversation starter that I can offer you is the conviction that caring communication with your son begins with mindful self-awareness to your own reactions that get triggered by your son's apparent difficulties.

When we as adults get anxious about what boys are not saying in words, we need to attend compassionately, in the moment, to our own reactions. What stories do we tell ourselves that keep us from being fully present with our children? By attending to our own inner worlds of thoughts, emotions, and even bodily sensations, we can be more attuned to a boy's emotional rhythms, and respect his ways of expressing himself, even through silence.

As you consider your son's stage of development, you might also find it helpful to know that it is typical for 10 year old boys in our culture to withhold information from their parents. In their developing autonomy, boys will experiment with shrugging off the guidance of loving parents. They want to feel strong and grown-up, and to appear unfazed as if trouble bounces off them. They may have internalized messages from the media and the wider culture that *real men* hide their feelings. ***Real men certainly*** do not cry.

It's possible that a 10 year old boy may assume that you don't need to be told what's up because you can read his mind. Since you have been caring for him his whole life, anticipating his changing needs, responding to his shifting moods, he may take it for granted that you have a sixth sense about his emotional world. He doesn't need to tell you everything. Perhaps he doesn't need to tell you anything.

But we ought not be taken in by a boy's distancing behaviour or attitude. Your son needs your attention more than he can ever say. He needs you to stay close when he is riddled with anger or anxiety. If he collapses and cries, he needs you to hold him, emotionally if not always physically. He may not be able to tell you why he's hurting, but he needs you to be calm and present with his pain.

Listen to What is Not Being Said

Given that about seventy-five percent of communication is non-verbal, how we respond to non-verbal messages—silence in particular—is critical. We want to listen to what is not being said as much as we listen to words. We have learned from much recent brain research that the brain attunes to deeper meanings by mirroring non-verbal messages. How often have we sent a silent message, ranging from "I love you" to "let's get out of here," to someone across the room? To understand the full meaning of what your son is saying or not saying, attend to his tone, the inflections in his voice, and especially his body language. By truly listening to what is not being said, we say to our children: "You are a person of worth. I love you, respect you, and want to understand you." Our own mirroring of non-verbal expressions might not speak to a boy's conscious brain, but it will speak to his deeper brain, helping him to recognize that we are on his side.

Give Full Attention

Most parents know that lectures, scolding, and advice are generally ineffective. When you want to communicate with your son, or make yourself available to him, make sure you are not preoccupied by other tasks, or distracted by the newspaper, TV, or Internet. Let go of any agendas as you turn toward him with a welcoming, receptive attitude. Be sensitive to his subtle cues. If you lean toward him with too much intensity, he may feel overpowered. If so, ease off to give him space. Notice whether or not he is comfortable with eye contact, and mirror his comfort level.

Tuning into a boy's sensitivities is quite different, of course, than doing things for him that he can in fact do for himself. Wise teachers and parents recognize that over-parenting, over-teaching, and over-protection can smother a boy's emerging independence. But we do not have to worry that we will make our boys weak by giving them too much nurturance or attention—as long as it is appropriate. Boys who are nurtured in their original families are better able to develop healthy attachments and a sense of social responsibility.

Acknowledge Your Son's Feelings

When we are anxious, we might at times, from the best of intentions, invalidate our children's feelings. "You don't really hate school," we might say, as if we would convince them their feelings are mistaken. We might follow this suggestion that we know them better than they know themselves with advice drawn from our wealth of useful experience, hardly noticing when their eyes glaze over. When a boy says, "My teacher yelled at me and everybody laughed," we might discount his feelings by quizzing: "What did you do to make your teacher so upset?"

Rather than appearing to take the teacher's side right away, we might simply mirror his feelings: "That hurts when we get laughed at" or even more simply, "That's hard." Less can be more when boys are reticent. Sometimes a simple acknowledgement of a child's feelings with a sincere "Oh….hmmm…. I see" is enough to help your son settle so he becomes open to discussion or self-exploration. We sometimes may worry that if we show empathy, children will think we're condoning their behaviour; however, acknowledging feelings does not mean we agree with what they did, or failed to do. Rather, it shows we care about their experience and their feelings. Once your son feels heard, you and he may be able to collaborate in thinking of ways he can avoid similar problems in the future.

Action-Talk

A boy's internal processing of thought and release of feelings often involves action—sometimes seen in his fidgeting, avoidance of eye contact, or quick bursts of energy, like slamming a door. When my mother noticed that I had pent up frustrations, she seemed to know that if she and I did something together—cutting up vegetables, walking, cleaning windows—I would be more relaxed than in a face-to-face encounter.

Frequently, when tempers flared in our house, my mother would send me out-of-doors to do a chore I enjoyed. Often she'd seek me out while I was in the middle of the chore, and work by my side, commenting briefly about what she imagined I was experiencing. When she mused aloud about the possible meaning of my non-verbal communication, sometimes I would respond. Sometimes I'd just be quiet. Respecting my need for quiet solitude, she simply planted a seedling thought for me to reflect on later.

In our home the tradition of playing simple games like *Crib* or *Yahtzee* at the kitchen table facilitated apparently casual, but surprisingly deep communication. I remember that when I was struggling inwardly, but not yet ready to talk, I'd find my way to the kitchen to play a game with whomever was hanging out in there. As we played and counted our way around the board in a game of *Crib*, I'd offer the odd comment about my struggle. Even when my internal world motored around like a washing machine stuck on the rinse cycle, my mother seemed to know just when to listen, when to ask a question, and when to offer a comment. I never felt pushed or prodded.

As you read the two dialogues between a parent and a son below, imagine yourself in the parent's place and notice your internal reactions.

Do you feel tempted to use more words to get the boy to talk?

Are you tempted to fix the problem? To offer advice?

Dialogue One: Friendship Loss

Son: "Billy moved away (looks forlorn). I had no one to play with today."

Dad: He moved away? Your best buddy?"

Son: (Eyes become watery) "He was the best friend I've ever had."

Dad: "Hmmm…. That hurts."

Son: "It sucks that we can't play street hockey now."

Dad: "That's really tough. You feel really sad about Billy moving away."

Son: (long pause, then suddenly his energy shifts) "What's for snack?"

Dad: "I'm guessing it's been a long day, and you need some grub…let's see…"(looks in the refrigerator for a few moments)… "We've got apples, cheese, peanut butter…."

(Son grabs an apple and a slice of cheese. He turns his back, heading for the front door. Dad watches him leave, resisting the impulse to say more)

Later that day, at bedtime…

Dad: "I've been thinking about Billy—you guys sure used to have a lot of fun together."

Son: (looks down and pauses for several seconds) "Yeah… we did."

Dad: "Remember the time you both went to *Laser Tag*? I remember watching the two of you run around. You were a great team."

Son: "Yeah…I know" (quickly closes his eyes and pulls the blanket over his head).

Dad: "It can be really hard when someone we like so much moves away."

Son: (silence at first, then begins to cry softly under the blanket)

Dad: "That friendship's meant a lot to you, son."

Son: (still under blanket, crying gently)

Dad: "I'm here. You can talk or not talk, whatever you feel like."

Son: (muffled) "I don't wanna talk."

Dad: "I've had friends move away too, so I can guess how painful this must be for you."

Son: (Silence. Still under blanket, not looking at Dad)

Dad: "If it's okay with you, I'll just stay a bit longer. Just so you know you're not alone right now."

Son: (silent under covers for several minutes while Dad sits quietly)

Dad: (after five or so more minutes brings closure to conversation) "Hey buddy—(touches the top of son's head, lightly stroking his hair for a couple of seconds)—" I guess I gotta get to bed myself. Any chance I could have a hug?"

Son: (Pulls covers down and quickly gives his dad a kiss and a hug, then just as quickly pulls the blanket back over his head)

Dialogue Two: Angry Outburst for no Obvious Reason

Son: Strides into the living room after school, throws backpack down on the sofa, falls onto sofa with look of aversion: "School sucks. Mr. Lucas is such a loser."

Mom: Observes quietly from the doorway, waits for more.

Son: (feels around for the TV remote control under the seat cushion, gives up in disgust) "No one ever puts stuff away in this house. It's impossible to live like this."

Mom: (Waits a few moments, then walks over, perching on the arm of a chair near her son) "Tough day, huh?"

Son: "Like he even knows anything about Geography. He is SUCH a STUPID IDIOT!"

Mom: "You're frustrated with your teacher?"

Son: "No kidding!"

Mom: "I'm guessing you're angry about something that happened in school...?"

Son: (Body stiffens as he sits in silence)

Mom: "I'm wondering if you're disappointed about a grade you got—or whether there's something going on you feel like talking about?"

Son: Silence

Mom: "Seems you don't feel like talking."

Son: (sits with hunched shoulders, looking down in silence)

Mom: "You look like something's on your mind."

Son: (silence)

Mom: "I don't know what's brought you down today, but I'll stay here a while in case you feel ready to talk."

Son: (Shoulders seem to relax as he continues with silence)

Mom:	(sits quietly near him while son looks unseeingly out the window for a few minutes)
Son:	(After this silence, son gets up and turns on the television manually while asking about the time)
Mom:	"It's 5:00. I have to get back to making dinner now. I'd appreciate it if you could set the table during the first commercial."
Son:	"Sure, Mom."
Mom:	"Maybe we can talk about this later. I'll check back with you" (smiles encouragingly).
Son:	(still silent, but glances at her without rancour before returning his gaze to the TV)

Just as perfect parenting is a myth, so is perfect listening. Listening is less about following rules for evoking particular responses and more about being self-aware and trusting that in your own creative and intuitive way you will be able to connect with your son. When boys are listened to, they learn, eventually, they don't have to manage their feelings by shutting others out or keeping their own feelings under wraps. Take comfort in the recognition that as your son learns to attend to his own inner world more fully without feeling pressured, he will learn to open up more. As you and other caring people are able to stay compassionate and present even when you don't know what exactly is going on, he will learn to become more present to himself and thus to others. As Scott Peck says in his book *The Road Less Travelled*, "More often than not, the most healing thing that we can do with someone who is in pain, rather than trying to get rid of that pain, is to sit there and be willing to share it."

5   Sibling Rivalry Beyond Cain & Abel

MOST parents of more than one child know that siblings fight. They may have heard a child yelling, "Mom! He's got my board again!" or "Dad! He's taken my cell phone!" It doesn't matter whether you're driving the kids to school, cutting up vegetables in the adjoining kitchen, or calmly watching the unfolding drama from the sofa; there really is no way to be absolutely sure who did what to whom. Often, feeling it's our job to do something, we may be overly zealous to reproach the one—often the oldest—whom we imagine to be the instigator, then soon discover that our reactions have made matters worse. The innocent victim now wears a smug smile, while the other child smoulders with anger, just waiting for a chance to balance the scales.

Sibling conflict is not always what it appears to be. One child may goad the other with subtle, almost invisible teasing; another may use more overt aggression. It can be hard, even for parents with front row seats, to tell who started what. The following email outlines a parent's struggle to make sense of her boys' bickering that will be familiar to many readers.

How do you respond to sibling conflicts when they are driving you crazy?

Dear Barry,

My two boys are driving me crazy with their incessant fighting and jealousy. I recall the warmth and hope I felt for our family the day we brought little Jacob home to meet his brother Daniel, who was almost 2, anticipating their growing friendship.

I honestly thought that having them close in age would benefit them, thinking that they'd get to experience so many wonderful things together. Boy, was I in for a surprise. It seems like they have been at odds from the get-go. I worry about the strain their rivalry is having on our family, especially during those few precious hours at the end of the day when we have the opportunity to be together.

Occasionally they can be the best of friends, but that is rare.

They are 8 and 10 years old now and they still quarrel about everything—toys, sports, bedtimes, chores, privacy, bossiness, television shows, neighbourhood friendships, personal appearances, and school grades.

I am particularly flabbergasted when they clash over computer time. Unlike his quieter brother Daniel, Jacob much prefers rambunctious outdoor play to electronic games, but they still have battles over computer time.

I am exhausted from trying to play referee.

My husband says it is normal for brothers to fight, that fighting could even be good for them. Of course, that's easy for him to say when he works longer hours, so it's mainly up to me to get the evening meal on the table after my own day at work. Interestingly, the moment he walks through the door at dinnertime, the boys' arguments intensify.

It's possible that my husband is right when he says that growing up with no brothers and one sister five years older than I was, I was not prepared for boys' conflicts. Still, I worry I am not doing enough, and that these daily fights will grow into lifelong hostility.

Why do they argue when I most need their cooperation? How can I help them get along better?

Clara

Dear Clara,

Most parents who have two or more children have become attuned to that moment when, from the other room, playful or excited laughter turns into whining, or angry shouts, or screams or crashes.

Nobody can push emotional buttons like a sibling.

Historically, parent experts have claimed that sibling rivalry is inevitable and that we ought to leave children to work it out.

Now many parents, educators, and researchers are questioning whether leaving kids to sort out their own conflicts is sufficient.

Even though your boys' fights are driving you around the bend, it is true that a certain amount of conflict is inevitable. After all, we can't change our siblings the way we can change our friends, so it is likely that the conflicts with our siblings will be more intense than with friends at times. In addition, conflict can teach children about respecting the needs of others as well as asserting their own needs.

However, I suspect that just as we have become uncomfortably aware of how we once turned a blind eye to playground bullying, we will soon recognize that ignoring the fights of siblings is not adequate.

Could it be that sibling conflict is more complex than we thought?

New research offered in ***Child Develpment*** entitled ***How Siblings Resolve Their Conflicts*** shines a light on sibling conflict, offering fresh perspectives for your consideration:

- on average, young siblings argue or fight 3 to 4 times an hour, and that the length of the conflicts varies, but the average is about 10 minutes per hour or about fifteen percent of the time

- about 1 out of every 8 conflicts ends in compromise or reconciliation —the other 7 times, the siblings merely withdraw, usually after the older child has bullied or intimidated the younger

- children make 7 times as many negative and controlling statements to their siblings as they do to their friends

- children are more likely to fight about sharing physical possessions or claiming them as their own than competition for parental attention

Before considering how you might reduce their rivalry without robbing your boys of the healthy opportunity to work it out between themselves, I suggest that you consider possible reasons for your boys' competition and conflicts. Time and time again I have witnessed parents and teachers make assumptions about children's behaviour and jump too quickly to expedient remedies.

Often, however, there can be reasons for children's behaviour that are not obvious, and which, if understood, would call for a different response.

Developing and Changing Needs

It's typical for kids' shifting developmental needs to affect how they relate to one another. Assertive 3 year olds and bossy 5 year olds can be a nasty mix. When Jacob was 3 and learning to assert his will, he may have been very protective of his toys and belongings and likely reacted aggressively to Daniel's domineering interest in his possessions. In turn, Daniel may have been trying out his own developing sense of autonomy as he entered kindergarten, practicing bossiness over his younger brother. Now that they are older and Daniel will soon be experimenting with increased independence as a teenager, he might resent being asked to take care of Jacob and play with him.

When someone new moves into a seat you thought was yours, jealousy is an all too human response. While it is likely that parents such as you and your husband were able to take the time to help the older child adjust to the arrival of a new infant, this jealousy dynamic can also occur within blended families. I'll not forget the reactive anger of one 10 year old boy when he lost his place as the eldest of three brothers, and suddenly became the middle child of five children, with the two step-siblings above him only a bit older than he was. Even with the most amicable divorce in the world, a child like this is losing, at least temporarily, his sense of place and identity.

We all want a place of security, and will challenge whatever appears to threaten our place in the world.

Everyday Practical Concerns

Daily stressors can drive children to take out their irritations and anger on a sibling. Lack of food or sleep can trigger a grouchy disposition. Over the past twenty years children have been sleeping less and less, with a third of children now suffering from inadequate sleep. Evidence suggests that children who sleep more get better grades. It is easy to hypothesize that sleep deprivation can also manifest as behavioural symptoms rather than obvious tiredness. In addition, a child who feels vulnerable over something parents might see as relatively small—changing a bedroom, starting on a sports team—might act out more with a sibling who is an available witness, dueling partner—or scapegoat.

Just as every teacher knows that the day after Halloween or the week before Christmas must be carefully planned, parents might consider how daily frustrations and unmet needs can swell their children's animosity toward one another.

Dietary Concerns

Is it possible that one or both of your boys' argumentative posturing before dinner could be related to nutritional deficiencies, dehydration, or even food allergies? Perhaps the boys need slower-burning protein foods at breakfast, recess, and lunch rather than the fast-burning carbohydrates and sugars so common to quick snacks and meals. Are the boys drinking enough water rather than processed fizzy drinks? We know from brain science that the brain needs lots of water to function at its optimum. If you suspect a dietary concern, seek the advice of a family doctor or a naturopathic physician to consider whether your boys' battles are fuelled by sensitivities to wheat, dairy, sugar, artificial colours and additives, or something else.

Consider trying the following experiment if you are a person who rarely drinks coffee or limits yourself to only one cup per day: Have several cups before your next monthly strata council committee meeting. I suspect that you will have a first-hand experience of how diet can make it difficult for us to manage conflict.

Individual Temperaments

Temperament can explain why a boy who is not afraid of playing street hockey can suddenly become terrified to visit *Chuck E Cheese*. Your boys' individual personalities and ability to adapt to others will affect how they get along. Daniel's quieter, more introspective temperament may be rattled by Jacob's rambunctious and outgoing nature. Alternatively, if Daniel is more sensitive than Jacob and seeks you out for comfort more frequently, Jacob might see his brother as a rival who is taking attention that should be going his way. Similarly, if Jacob has some sort of learning issue requiring more parental time, Daniel might pick up on this disparity and act out to get attention. Sometimes one child's perfectionist tendencies clash with the other child's relaxed temperament, or one child's impetuosity goes against the grain of a more cautious sibling.

Parental Role Modelling

Consider how you and your husband manage individual stress as well as disagreements you may have as a couple. Children will pick up on your stress, and will likely emulate your ways of managing, sidestepping, or escalating conflict.

Do your kids hear you talking about anger at a co-worker, worrying out loud about a relative's illness, or arguing with a spouse about financial matters? Kids are often sponges for their parents' anxieties and frustrations. You might assume that you are cleverly hiding your own frustrations as a couple, but it is during times of heightened stress that childrens' antennaes tune in. When parents work through conflict in ways that are respectful rather than blaming, calmly assertive rather than aggressive, they increase the chances that kids will adopt similar habits when they run into problems with one another. When kids routinely observe us shout and slam doors, or sulk and withdraw when differences arise, they're likely to pick up those habits too.

Family Atmosphere

Parents establish a certain tone or atmosphere in the home that can enhance or cloud sibling relationships. When expectations are unclear, absent, or inconsistent, kids may become anxious about what is expected, and then vent their anxieties through squabbles with a sibling. A rigid or overly authoritarian family atmosphere can challenge kids to rebel, especially kids who are Daniel's age or older.

If you are not familiar with Dorothy Law Nolte's poem, **Children Learn What They Live,** it might be helpful for you and your husband to read the poem together and consider what you may be reinforcing in your home.

Time and Performance Pressures

We no longer have to wait till adulthood in order to feel over-committed and overwhelmed. In many cases, we seem to be acculturating our children to be burdened by schedules and too much busyness that they are unable to relax after school or play creatively. These kids may begin to seek inappropriate ways to release that stress. Children who signal they feel overscheduled by complaining about the number of activities they're involved in or refusing to go to them may express their frustrations in their sibling politics.

Stress Outside of The Home

School, sports teams, and music lessons usually help children learn new skills and make new friends. However, in some cases, stress outside the home, even through activities that are supposedly good for them, can be a source of frustration that leads to crankier sibling interaction. If either of your boys becomes more irritable or more withdrawn than usual, consider whether they may be overwhelmed by pressures associated with a teacher, a coach, or a schoolyard bully.

A recent study in the **British Journal of Developmental Psychology** found that schoolyard bullies are more likely to bring bullying behaviours home to their siblings. The study found that significantly more boys than girls bully their younger sibling, and that kids with an older male sibling were the most victimized group.

Another current study established that sixty percent more boys are likely to require psychiatric care during their teen years if they were bullies or frequent victims in earlier years, and even greater if they were both a victim and bully. The study also notes that increased childhood bullying is linked to increased depression and suicidal thinking among teenage males.

Responding to Sibling Rivalry

As you consider the ways in which your boys' sibling conflicts may be fuelled by circumstances that go beyond the obvious, I encourage you to reflect on the underlying reasons for their excessive conflict that you might not yet have considered. I also suggest that you reduce the amount of time you spend refereeing their differences and avoid taking sides or playing detective with them. Specifically, you might try saying the following in a calm and assertive manner the next time their tempers go through the roof: "This isn't working," and send them to separate rooms for about ten minutes. Sometimes it's best just to give them space for a little while rather than immediately trying to rehash the conflict. If you want to help them to learn from their experience, wait until the emotions have calmed; otherwise their conflict is likely to escalate into blaming and yelling again. Be careful to not stare or look at either one of your boys in particular, as it is easy to unconsciously look to the child we perceive as the instigator, unintentionally feeding their perception that we are taking sides.

Do your best to appreciate each child for who he is, and do not compare or typecast your children. It's not too surprising when Lisa, in *The Simpsons*, is the brain in the family, that Bart will define his identity as a troublemaker. Take time, whatever you can manage, to spend with each child alone, and he will be less likely to feel a strong need to separate himself from his sibling to gain attention from you.

When your children do fight, your own calm and relaxed response will be a model for your boys' interactions. And knowing how we all like to be appreciated, take the time to notice the occasions that they do cooperate and behave like the best of friends. This noticing of their brotherly friendship will also go a long way to help you maintain your own positive perspective—and sanity!

6   Sibling Rivalry—Finding a Point of Balance

WE know that siblings will have clashing goals and desires at time, and some conflict is simply a measure of being alive, and being in relationship. We know from our own lives that suppressing frustration and anger too much can dampen our life force. We hope that our children will learn from sibling conflicts to disagree respectfully, to listen and work out differences without losing sight of their own needs and desires.

There are no ready-made formulae to deal with children's fights. Each family is different. Below you will find several suggestions to help you avoid some common pitfalls parents fall into when they are trying to sort out sibling conflicts.

How can you increase the chances that children will benefit from the conflicts in the family crucible?

Dear Barry,

Now that I have figured out why my kids go on and on about the littlest disagreements and have become generally less involved with asking, "Who started it?" I really would appreciate some more ideas to help me curb their rivalry and aggression toward each other.

My mom always said that "kindness begins in the home" and I recognize that ultimately it is my job as their parent to teach them important life skills. Still, I can't help but wonder if there is more I can do to encourage them to live more harmoniously in my family.

Mei

Dear Mei,

Establish Rules for Privacy and Personal Possessions

Since many fights between siblings are about possession, take time to discuss privacy issues with children on a regular basis. All family members can collaborate to establish ground rules for *stuff*. When children share a room and fight over possessions, it can be helpful for both children to have identified designated spaces that are their own, clearly off bounds to the other. Make it clear that each child needs to respect the other's possessions and privacy.

If conflict about possessions continues to erupt, show your faith that the kids can work things out themselves. It can also help to calm and interrupt the cycle of mounting agitation if you say something like, "I see that you both want the *DS* right now. I believe that you can find a solution that can work for both of you. Let me know what you come up with."

Establish Rules for Conflict

Children need to know that hitting, yelling, and damaging property are not acceptable. Without rules for fighting fair, small disagreements and disturbing insults can easily escalate to volcanic levels within a relatively short period of time.

Evidence indicates that persistent harassment and physical assault can have long-lasting effects on the relationship between siblings. Evidence also indicates that bullying can be as addictive as nicotine, as the brain of a person who is bullying receives a chemical high. In addition, we know that the longer a child is allowed to continue to bully a sibling, the greater the likelihood that the child bully will eventually become an adult bully. The neural networks formed in childhood and reinforced through practice and feedback can become so hardwired that they are difficult to change later.

Your kids should also know that there can be moments when an agreement to disagree is the best strategy. Teach them how to bring closure to a disagreement with a simple exit statement such as, "You see it your way and I see it my way. Let's take a break for now."

Avoid Taking Sides

As each child tries to convince you of the righteousness of his position, re-member that playing judge or taking sides will probably feed their conflict and animosity. Instead, you might say, "It's okay for you to disagree. I'm sure you can work it out. Follow our family rules for fighting fair." If the fight escalates too much, you might send them to separate places until their arousal level calms, and they can come back together to work things out. Remember that yelling, scolding, and threatening to stop fights can create a diverting or entertaining drama that may energize the very behaviours that you want to see stopped.

Intervene in Low-key Ways

Just as *Boy Smarts: Mentoring Boys for Success at School* describes how gender exists along a continuum, so do parental responses to sibling conflict. At extremes we can be overly strict, trying to control their fights by grabbing at rewards and punishments. "If you don't stop fighting, you're both grounded for a month!" At the other end of the spectrum we can be overly permissive, ignoring the fighting altogether. How do we find a place of balance?

Even the wisest, most experienced parents may struggle with the question of whether to remain on the sidelines or intervene in a conflict.

If a conflict seems to be escalating into a red danger zone, you may consider what might have contributed to the heightened agitation. Might there be physical or emotional factors such as hunger, lack of sleep, trouble at school? If you observe that they are both tired, you could help them toward more self-awareness and defuse confrontation by saying, "You're both tired. It might be best to take some time apart." If you try to calm them with words such as "Easy does it, you two," be mindful that your own tone is easy, neutral and calm; any agitation in your own voice is likely to add to combustion.

Be aware that closer supervision is usually needed for pre-schooler siblings than older siblings, especially if one child is more aggressive than the other.

When younger siblings are hounding each other on a boring, rainy day, sideline their conflict by pulling out a special game held in reserve for such occasions. The novelty will likely intrigue them.

Give Feedback Where Necessary

Sometimes it may be important to communicate concerns privately to the child who repeatedly tattles or is caught in a harmful pattern of provoking the other. There's a much better chance of improved behaviour if you avoid correcting your son in front of siblings. When you quietly take one child aside to help him get back on track avoid discussing blame and focus on solutions. Be firm in your insistence that you will not tolerate fighting that violates the family rules. Have the conversation soon after the offending behaviour occurs, but at a time when heads are cool and problems can be discussed sensibly. Show patience and acceptance. Let your child know that while the solution is negotiable, your expectation of their behaviour is not: The behaviour has to stop. You'll likely need to listen to his complaints about his sibling as the deeper issue surfaces.

Keep in mind that as kids learn to cope with their disputes, they'll also learn important skills that will serve them for life: how to value differing perspectives, and how to negotiate, how to compromise, and how to manage aggressive impulses.

Avoid Expectations that Fuel Resentment

Avoid telling your eldest that he should know better or that it is his job to teach his younger brother to get along. The eldest is likely to feel resentment about being saddled with the responsibility to caretake the younger, and the younger may feel disempowered by the suggestion that he needs to be taken care of. When we set siblings up to become rivals through comparisons, they will be less likely to help each other later on.

Remember that your children will have different friends and they shouldn't have to share friends unless they want to. Younger siblings often intrude on older siblings' friendships and play. Distract and redirect the younger sibling with a playmate or special activity when your older child has a friend over.

Avoid Comparisons and Typecasting

Comparisons can fuel competition for your attention and build acrimony: "Look how Colin sits quietly at the dinner table. Why can't you do the same?" or "Why can't you eat everything on your plate like Colin does?"

Children need to know that they are loved for who they are and that each brings something special to the family. Take care to appreciate their differing strengths by honouring their distinctive personalities and encouraging each to pursue interests and passions—such as their choices in sports, books, movies, or games.

Try not to lump them together, even in moments of exasperation. See your children as separate beings, and, at the same time, avoid giving them labels that they may become straitjackets for their identity. Labels such as *Slowpoke, Nerd, Social Butterfly,* and *Black Sheep* can become self-fulfilling prophecies. Even neutral or positive labels such as the *Family Jock* or the *Brain* may send the message that one child has a monopoly on sports, and the other the monopoly on school smarts.

Understand that it's not possible to treat them both exactly the same way as their differing needs warrant differing responses and differing kinds of support. Do not fall into the trap of assuming that you must do exactly the same thing for each child. No matter how hard you try to make things equal, children are bound to find something that's unfair. Let children know the family resources will be used to meet the needs of family members in different ways at different times. Children feel more secure and happy knowing that we can love and treat each differently, and that there is abundant caring and kindness for everyone.

Help Children Discern Between Telling and Tattling

Recently, I had the opportunity to speak to several classrooms of Grade 5 to 7 students in three different school communities about bullying. I was surprised to learn that the majority of students struggled to delineate everyday teasing from harmful bullying and did not believe that teachers or parents would help them if they complained. Further discussion revealed that they were also unable to identify the difference between tattling and telling. Despite our desire for children to speak up when they are hurt or in trouble, I can't help but wonder if we may be confusing them when we respond with mixed messages such as: "Stop tattling about your brother," or "I don't want to hear about it."

Recognize that tattling can provide an alternative to name-calling and physical fighting by allowing the unskilled child a face-saving excuse to exit conflict: "I'm going to tell on you." Tattling can also reveal a child's desire to show you that he understands right from wrong: "Logan hit me." Still, it can be difficult for younger kids to make judgments about what's tattle-worthy and what isn't. Parents can help children understand that some issues are serious, and should be taken to a responsive adult who can help. Unlike this kind of telling, tattling is motivated by the desire for revenge, the desire to get someone into trouble. You want to discourage this kind of manipulative behaviour.

Explain to your children that it's okay to alert you when someone is hurt or may become hurt, but not okay to tell if they are trying to get someone into trouble. Since kids may still have trouble differentiating dangerous behaviour from annoying behaviour, asking a simple question like, "In trouble or out of trouble?" may help them learn to distinguish between the two. While ensuring that everyone is safe, you might also help your child explore his own motivations by asking questions such as "What happened? What did you want to have happen? Are there any ways you could work it out yourselves?" While you don't want to bury your head in the sand, you also want to avoid getting drafted repeatedly into the role of conflict mediator. Ideally you want your kids to become increasingly independent in learning to assess fraught situations, and work toward resolution.

When children distinguish between tattling and telling in the early years, they will be more likely to seek adult guidance later on when potential danger arises.

Listen When Calm

If kids have had the time to become calm and still want to talk about their frustrations, take time to listen to their story. When they are still very bothered by what has been happening with a sibling, they might be reaching out for help. Helping them work through their feelings and explore ideas will most certainly be slower than issuing an ultimatum and demanding obedience, but will go much further toward helping to illuminate underlying issues and prepare the ground for true resolution.

While paying for groceries the other day, I overheard an exasperated parent try to talk her son out of his feelings by saying, "Stop complaining. He's the only brother you have." In such moments kids often become calmer not by having us agree that they are truly victimized, but simply by having us show empathy, seeing and validating their feelings of frustration: "Sounds like you're really angry right now."

When Sibling Conflict is Too Much, Speak About Your Own Feelings and Needs

Knowing our own emotional patterns can help everyone find a way to modulate their emotions before a fight gets out of control. If we choose to let our own impatience build and build, intervening only after a fight has peaked, we may over-react ourselves. If sibling fights are interfering with your ability to function, let your kids know how their behaviour is affecting you: "I'm trying to cook dinner, and your fight is interrupting me from getting dinner on the table. I need some peace, so I'd like you to find another place to work out your differences, or let it go for now."

If they are arguing over the sharing of a toy electronic game, you might also give them one minute to work it out or the toy will be put away—chances are they would rather play together than have the toy removed.

Because the backseat of the car can be an endless battle zone, recognize that boredom is usually the culprit. Ensure that there are plenty of things for them to do when they are in the car. If they do fight and make it difficult for you to concentrate on driving, pull over. You might say quietly that you don't feel safe driving when you feel distracted by their fighting. Wait quietly for them to stop as you manage your own frustration.

Remember that telling a child to not do something works best when it is followed by a positive option: "You may not scream or hit your brother, but you may walk away or go someplace quiet." Recognize that when an argument is brewing, early intervention can help siblings begin to learn skills in coping with conflict: "If you talk quietly, you will be more likely to solve your problem."

Teach and Model How to Listen

When you do decide, after reflection, to become involved in your kids' conflict, help them clarify what they are arguing about by showing them how to listen better. Ask each child to describe the problem from their point of view for a minute or two, while the other child listens without any interruption. If they still don't understand the issue, try to describe it for them. Be cautious to not reveal your bias, with excessive eye contact perhaps. Unless there's an obvious culprit, do not try to decide who is to blame, who started it, or who is right. Be aware that interrogating them about their conflict can be counterproductive, as it may encourage them to exaggerate or lie to avoid consequences. Adults may think that they are teaching right from wrong when they use interrogation to get to the bottom of a problem, but grilling usually causes people to justify and harden their position. Finally, avoid imposing a solution which they have not helped to discover: after all, it's their problem, and you will not always be around to adjudicate. Besides, the more you intervene, the more you will be called upon to intervene.

Make Time Alone For Each Child

Make one-on-one time a priority when conflict seems more frequent than usual. Bedtime is often a good opportunity for children to have some time alone with you. Recognize that when school or daycare has been upsetting, children need your complete attention to debrief, distress, and reconnect with you. A couple of minutes spent talking and sharing about each other's day can go a long way toward calming or even averting an emotional storm.

Keep a Long-range Perspective

As you apply these strategies, remember that perfect families do not exist. Fights between children do not necessarily augur a lifetime of bitterness. Siblings who rarely fight may end up in distant, cold relationships down the road, while siblings who engage in conflict often grow much closer over time, especially when there are more good times than bad.

7   Fostering Peace on the Home Front

IN recent months parents have emailed me conveying their anxiety over the impulsivity and aggression they have seen in their boys—and especially in sibling conflicts that just keep escalating rather than quietly going away.

How can you support positive relationships between siblings from the very beginning and teach boys peacemaking skills?

Dear Barry,

I understand what you are saying about giving siblings space to work through their disagreements while also stepping in to give them a helping hand at times, but I wonder about the influence that our couple conflict has. As my husband's voice is much louder than mine, I especially worry that our couple quarrels may inadvertently be fueling their emotional upset and tantrums toward one another.

When I describe our couple conflicts to my counsellor, she says that they are common—even reasonable—and that it is also quite typical for 4 and 6 year old boys to be like warriors on the prowl. I accept that I should expect more boisterous sibling hullabaloo than my own childhood upsets with my sister, yet I would like to teach my boys to also be peaceful warriors. Suggestions?

Anne

Dear Anne,

Whether they live with a single parent, the traditional mom and dad, an extended family, or another of the many other possible combinations, boys are constantly observing and learning from adult patterns of speech and behaviour.

Studies reveal that in homes where conflict is intense, children become more aggressive. They also become ill more frequently, have more depression and anxiety, and more sleep problems than children who come from homes with less conflict. At the same time, brushing conflicts under the rug is not healthy either. Children who rarely see conflict being worked through may learn to shy away from any form of disagreement; later they may find it easier to go along with peer pressure than resist it. Children copy the patterns of interaction that they observe—whether it is demeaning criticism, threats, or eruptions of rage—or healthy ways to manage anger and resolve conflict respectfully.

While children need not know the intimate details of a parental conflict, let them see that you and your partner are committed to working through differences, even when you agree to postpone discussing a sore point until later. Since many children tend to worry when they don't know the outcome, be sure to let them know later when your conflict has been resolved.

Male Adult Role Models

Both parents have critical roles in helping siblings learn to get along with each other, but as gender role models, fathers are especially well positioned to teach boys how to manage their emotions and aggression. From their own boyhood experiences, men know that boys in play may turn sticks into guns, but fantasy play is not reality, and very few boys confuse the two after the age of 6 or 7. Most fathers also understand that it is not possible, or productive, to try to insulate boys from all fantasy enactments of violence.

Fathers can help boys develop the empathy that is the best inhibitor of real life violence that hurts others. Through modelling compassion in their communication with their sons, fathers can help their sons internalize a compassionate outlook toward others. When what may have started as rough-and-tumble play ends up crossing into a zone of harm, fathers can show their sons how to interrupt a cycle that is getting out of control, backing off, soothing hurt feelings, perhaps noting calmly that it's time for a break. On the sports field fathers can also help by helping boys see the big picture; they can encourage boys whose egos have been bruised in competition: "Shake it off, Matthew. We'll get it back" or "I saw how you're really working to pass the puck."

As all wise parents know, too much emphasis on competition with the goal of winning can exacerbate sibling rivalry.

Fathers would be wise to understand that if playtime with their son is always competitive and rambunctious, boys may assume that dads are for rough play, and moms are for gentle interaction. Fathers can ensure that they foster balanced relationships with their sons by taking time to:

- share calm snuggle-time on the sofa with a book, reading together
- develop a routine for hellos and goodbyes, cherishing loving moments of connection
- name your emotions and admit your stress, along with your plan to manage stress
- show your sadness and vulnerability, not just your anger or frustration (Let your boy see you cry)
- listen to your son when he wants to tell you something by giving your son full attention, looking at him with warmth and interest
- mention small, positive things that you see him doing, whether it is getting ready for school on time, sharing candy with a sibling, backing off from a potential fight, or phoning home when he said he would
- take time to inquire about the best and the worst thing that happened during the day
- correct gently by keeping your voice calm and level
- help boys to start each day with positive input, knowing that a hand on the shoulder, or loving words can help boys who are struggling, and strengthen them throughout the day

Fathers should also be aware that studies show that the emotional support the first child gets from the father during the early years may be a significant factor in the relationship between the two children in later years.

Through play and sensitive discussion with the first-born child, dads can take extra time to teach coping skills while mom is attending to the newborn, helping the oldest to understand that he still has a place of worth and value in his growing family.

Of course, since some boys do not have a father in their lives, it can be helpful in such cases to seek out other mature male role models for our sons. We can all appreciate the valuable role men in the community perform as teachers, coaches, and concerned neighbours. By exposing boys to a variety of men who talk explicitly about their values, their emotions, and even their struggles, we give boys more choice about different possibilities for the kinds of men they want to be.

Men can teach boys that a man can be open to self-understanding as well as deep empathy toward others; that manhood is not defined by the media or street culture, but is instead defined by a set of core loving values.

Teach Siblings How to Be Assertive

If we want boys to learn to apply the brakes on aggression in appropriate ways, they will need to learn how to be assertive with their sibling without being aggressive. Take time to explain strategies by which they might assert their needs and boundaries, saying something like, "Stop. Don't do that," or "I don't like it when you do that. I'm going to play elsewhere." If you have both children on board and are able to explore peacemaking strategies with them, you might even suggest a code that one can use if the play fight has gone too far: "Red light!"

Other strategies to call a halt in an assertive way include:

Call time out—When anger, hurt, or other strong emotions are rumbling, call time out. You can return later to the conflict when the arousal level is calmed for both parties.

Without yelling, say what you are feeling with a bold, firm voice—"This is hurting. I want to stop."

Without ultimatums or threats, say what you want to happen—"I want to have a turn too."

Sometimes Tantrums Are a Cry for Help

When temper tantrums flare during a sibling conflict, respond with calmness. Ignoring the tantrum, or shouting harshly, "Stop that now or I'll give you something to cry about!" are extreme responses that teach children that their feelings don't count. Recognize that a child indulging in a temper tantrum is often tired, hungry, or very, very frustrated. In such moments boys need us to demonstrate a calm response, something like: "I know that you are frustrated (or hungry, or tired, or all three) right now. Just take a moment to breathe and relax. It's okay. We'll work it out." When he is calm, you can talk about how he might express his feelings without screaming, stomping, or slamming the door. Instead of labelling your son as selfish when he is reluctant to share, try to help your child to imagine how the sibling feels. A child who learns to look at his anger with your support and compassion can begin to develop self-understanding, perhaps eventually even learning that the anger is a mask for other feelings such as hurt, embarrassment, or sadness. This compassion toward the self is where compassion for others is born.

Name and Discuss Emotional Triggers

Boys, who have been taught by the culture to appear tough, controlling, and disconnected from their feelings, often express their strong emotions through actions rather than words. Some boys slam a door, hit a wall, or even punch something hard because they don't know how to verbalize their emotions.

Compared to girls, boys between the ages of 6 to 14 years old commonly struggle with communication:

- for every 100 girls with speech difficulty, 214 boys have speech difficulty.

- for every 100 girls with difficulty hearing conversation, 149 boys have difficulty hearing conversation.

Boys need support to learn ways to identify their feelings so that they do not become swept away by a torrent of strong emotions. Boys who explode in anger may not yet be able to identify what their anger is all about. They need support as they learn to separate out their feelings and their thoughts, and to identify triggers for their angry reactions: "Are you angry that he got to go first?"

Help boys to develop the habit of saying what they're feeling and why: "I'm angry because I have to vacuum while Sarah gets to go outside." Using words won't mean that he necessarily gets his way, but finding words to explain his feelings can help him to get settled enough to see more clearly.

When we manage our own adult anger in a clear, calm way by saying something like, "I am really angry when you two are yelling so loud. I am going to take a few minutes to settle myself upstairs and then we will talk about what happened," boys will learn that anger is natural and that it can be expressed and managed.

Teach boys to identify their own feelings by using *I statements*: I feel _____ when _____ because _____. For example, "I feel angry when Richard calls me crybaby because this name embarrasses me."

The practice of making *I statements* teach boys over time that emotions often underlie anger. In the preceding example, embarrassment—perhaps fear of being seen as silly—gave rise to the anger. Being able to step back when one is flushed with anger, look at what is going on underneath, and make a non-blaming *I statement* is an important step in learning to manage conflict.

Establish a Game Plan

Many boys start school lacking the ability to regulate their social and emotional behaviours. Researchers tell us that this problem with restraint and self-regulation has a stronger connection with later academic achievement than IQ, entry-level reading, or even math skills. Children who lack self-control are also at increased risk of developing troubled relationships with peers and teachers, another strong forecaster of academic difficulties and behaviour problems in later years.

Researchers have long believed that teaching self-control involves guiding children to plan how their play will unfold. This approach gets children to establish a plan of action for how they will use language BEFORE they even begin to play. It turns out that playing family games like *Simon Says* teaches children how they will apply the brakes of restraint.

It is important for children to practise the skill of waiting their turn even before they start school where there is so much waiting and turn-taking: waiting to answer until the teacher calls, waiting to touch something interesting during show-and-tell, waiting to play with an interesting gadget during a science lesson. Recognize that boys need to make a game plan for how they will manage their impulses when they want gratification now. Provide specific external language such as: "May I have a turn with that...?" or "I'm playing with the game now, but you may have it after lunch"; along with specific internal language such as: "Hang on. My turn will come," or "I can wait for a few more minutes."

Practise the Game Plan

When you are talking to someone and your son keeps interrupting, it is tempting to say, "Not now! I'm busy" and then forget to follow up. In fact, this is a chance for you to teach your son a new practice. Explain to him that you are going to try something new when he wants to talk to you and you're busy. Show him how to gently place his hand on your forearm as the signal to gain your attention without interrupting. In response, put your hand over his hand so he knows that you have seen his signal. Practise by pretending you are talking to someone and ask him to use the signal, prompting only as much as necessary. The moment he places his hand on your forearm, stop your conversation, gently place your free hand over his hand, and immediately ask him what he wants. You can then begin to extend the time between the signal and your response, but certainly try to respond as quickly as you can so your child learns an alternative to interrupting.

After you have experienced repeated success, apply the idea of establishing an advance game plan for cooperation between siblings during a family meeting. Start with an issue that evokes mild—not red hot—agitation between siblings. Recently, two boys told me about their plans: "We agreed to not take each other's hockey equipment without asking first…and to knock on each other's door and wait for permission to enter before barging in."

Family Meetings Teach Cooperation

When we tell children to not fight without teaching them how to make peace, we shouldn't be surprised that they default to fighting in times of high stress. Setting aside time each week to routinely discuss the ups and downs of family life will convey your commitment to peacemaking, shared decision-making, and democratic cooperation. During regular family meetings everyone should have the opportunity to offer an opinion and be heard.

Many families find it helpful to discuss the differences between acceptable levels of rumbling, and explosive conflict that goes too far. They might brainstorm strategies for recognizing when things are getting out of control, and calling a temporary halt. They might agree to ground rules for fighting fair such as no hitting, name-calling, yelling, or door-slamming. Your family might discuss how to decide whether permission is required to borrow someone's property, or when it is important to knock before entering a room. Family meetings can teach boys responsibility for their own actions, regardless of the situation or level of provocation. They can also head off any attempt to assign blame.

One family recently emailed about their family decision to insist on fair treatment for everyone: they posted a note on their fridge to remind them: "You can be angry with me, but you can't yell, hit, or put me down."

Another family emailed me with another meeting success story over managing rainy day conflicts with a *Boredom Box* that contained special items such as rarely played games, highly desirable books, and a surprise treat. Taking time to plan for potential problems helps boys to establish a plan of action and avert conflict.

Sustaining motivation for family meetings requires effort and imagination. You might decide that it can be fun to look for, acknowledge, and celebrate recent successes in reducing conflict and creating more peace. One family with 10 year old and 12 year old boys emailed me about a celebration where they strengthened solidarity during a *Wild Pizza* night, where they designed, baked and ate the most outrageous pizza each child could imagine—and stomach.

Remember to also take family meeting time to include an opportunity for everyone to express their appreciation for each other, knowing that these positive comments generate goodwill.

Family meetings will teach your children not only how to negotiate and get along better, but they will also teach them that it is possible to find solutions to everyday life problems.

Offer a Peacemaking Plan

Those of us who grew up with a brother or sister recognize that we can have a fierce loyalty bond with a sibling who is also a sworn adversary. Despite working hard to teach siblings how to get along, now and then children will still run into a conflict that will warrant your attention. Boys who can talk through their anger are less likely to act out in ways that harm others. With your help, most boys can be taught to manage conflict through the following peacemaking steps:

1. STOP conflict before someone gets hurt
2. Choose PEACE—step back and breathe deeply and slowly
3. When you are both ready, AGREE to solve the problem
4. Take turns to TELL what's bothering you—listen with eyes, ears and heart Use *I statements*
5. Think of ways to SOLVE the problem
6. Choose a PLAN for peace
7. Put the peace plan into ACTION

Too often we lecture boys, trying to stuff them full of advice. The following shows how a parent might apply the above model of peacemaking.

1. "STOP before someone gets hurt. I see that you are both getting very angry."

2. "I will hold on to the remote control while you both find PEACE by taking some time to breathe and become relaxed."

3. "The television will remain off until you both AGREE to solve your disagreement"

    (After a few minutes both children agree that they are ready to work out their disagreement.)

4. "Who wants to TELL and who listen first with eyes, ears, and heart?"

    (A three-minute egg timer that uses minute grains of sand work best because they are highly visual—to ensure that each manages the turn to the best of his or her ability.)

5. "Let's explore ways to SOLVE your problem."

    Depending on their experience with generating solutions you might need to offer suggestions.

    - We could set a timer and take turns.

    - You could have the remote before dinner and I could have the remote after dinner.

    - We could play with it together.

    - We could each toss a coin to see who gets the remote first.

    - We could put the remote away and leave the television off.

    - We could go outside and do something else.

6. "Which PLAN for peace can you both settle on?"

(Consider saying the following if it becomes clear that either needs more time to consider the peace options: If you won't agree on a plan for peace, we will take a break and try again in fifteen minutes," or "If you are not ready to agree on a plan for peace, I will keep the remote safe until after dinner.")

7. "Time to put your plan for peace into ACTION. Here's the remote and the timer. I'll check back in a little while to see how your plan is going."

Seek Consultation When Necessary

In a small percentage of families, the conflict between siblings can be so severe that it disrupts daily living and leaves a parent struggling on the verge of desperation. If this is the case in your family, it's wise to seek support from a *Registered Clinical Counsellor* who specializes in understanding families, conflict, and boys. Seek help for your children's conflict when it leads to marital problems; when it creates a real danger of physical harm to any family member; or when you suspect it may be related to other significant concerns, such as depression or serious drug use. Finally, seek support if one child feels left out because the sibling is extremely ill, disabled, or at risk, and the parents are necessarily preoccupied with meeting the needs of the one child for an extended period.

Tending the Hearth

Evidence has shown that when siblings learn to manage intense emotion and jealousy within their family, they will become better peacemakers on the playground, in the classroom, and later in life.

They are also likely to become each other's best friend down the road.

Learning to argue without hurting is an essential life skill. Those fortunate enough to have siblings can learn early on that their needs are not the only ones that count, and that different stories, and different versions of reality can exist simultaneously. Strong families help children learn that there is nothing mystical about good communication, that it is something that must be worked on, and there is no better person to practise with than a brother or sister. Mahatma Gandhi once said: "It is not this or another action which makes us peacemakers, but it is the entire fabric of our lives." It is for this reason that we should spend less time trying to put out random blazes on the home front, and more time tending the hearth by which we, and our children, warm ourselves.

8   Father Hunger

THE following email is from a father left reeling the aftermath of a divorce and struggling to forge a new relationship with his son. Like so many men who received poor fathering themselves when they were young, this father feels ill equipped to manage his own adult stress, let alone become a positive role model to his son. My response highlights the importance of boys' need for fathers—or, if no father is available to them, other men—to guide them in their journeys to manhood.

How can fathers forge a connection with their son, especially after divorce?

> **Dear Barry,**
>
> My wife and I recently divorced and I really need some coaching about how to be a better father to my only child, a boy who is 6 years old.
>
> As a guy I found it easy to listen to your talk the other night, and I really got your message that it is important for us dads to be more involved in our son's lives. Times have changed and so must we be more involved than our own fathers. Your comments spoke deeply to me.
>
> I barely know how to handle the stress in my own life, let alone teach my son how he could better deal with his own frustrations. My dad was hardly around when I was growing up. After my parents got divorced

when I was 10 he became even scarcer, always blaming everyone else for his problems and my mom for limiting visitations.

I was basically fatherless. I grew up insecure about myself. To top it off my father had a drinking problem and was a real *Jekyll and Hyde*. He rarely showed vulnerabilities or tender emotions at all, but he managed to let his anger rip. I remember eating my dinner in a hurry so that I could escape his yelling at my mom to go outside to play. I could never share my feelings or show any emotions to him at all. No one ever said this to me in plain words but somehow I came to believe that showing emotions was a sign of weakness. I mastered the art of running away from every conflict or fight. I know this is why my marriage failed.

I've moved away from the family home and lost the opportunity to make my relationship work with my son's mom, but I know it's not too late to be a better father to my son. I could really use your advice.

Cameron

Dear Cameron,

Divorce is a painful experience for all involved. There are many caring dads, like you, who struggle with the stress of divorce as well as their own lack of fathering, and long to become better men and healthier fathers with their own kids.

Life gives us numerous opportunities in key relationships to learn from our experiences, work out our differences, and pass on those legacies that are truly worthwhile.

You own life has taught you how boys look to their fathers to learn what a boy should become, what he should work to accomplish, or try to avoid. As boys grow older, they often learn how to outmanoeuvre their fathers in ways that do not always serve them later. Paradoxically, most sons also need acceptance and approval from the same men they seek to overcome.

We imagine it was often easier in the past for many fathers and sons to maintain strong attachments by sharing time, working on chores together, or sharing outdoor adventures. Still, we also know that the good old days were not always so good, filled with fathers patiently teaching boys practical and emotional skills in the woodshop or on the farm. Many fathers were harsh, or absent in their emotional connectivity with their sons, leaving boys feeling lost and confused as they struggled toward manhood, and eventually become fathers themselves.

When family life is interrupted by separation or divorce, it can be especially challenging for fathers and sons to maintain meaningful connections. Most of us know that fathers have a unique role in influencing and shaping their sons' lives. When fathers do not seek to maintain strong connections after a divorce, boys risk seeing very limited, one-dimensional versions of masculinity, not the full range of male behaviour. We also know that, regardless of family income, absent or negative father-son relationships are clearly linked to a host of problems among boys including underachievement, depression, violence, and substance abuse.

For a boy to reach a healthy version of manhood, his father and other significant men must allow their emotions to be visible—hardly an easy task when most males grow up being either subtly or openly taught that any emotions other than anger must not be shown. Boys need to learn that masculinity and emotional openness can go together.

As you get involved in your son's life and show him caring acceptance, he becomes less vulnerable to negative influences from peers or from media displays of hyper-masculinity.

If mentoring from a father is absent, inadequate, or marked by excessive emotional distance, boys can develop distorted views of themselves. If father hunger is too intense, a boy may assume the aggressive or exaggerated masculine identity of some TV or video game heroes. He may feel he can never be good enough, adequate enough, manly enough. He may distrust other males, fearing their criticism and abandonment.

Your son needs you to show him how to identify and express his thoughts and strong feelings in a climate of safety, especially when he is stressed and prone to lash out in frustration. Indeed, when boys see that their fathers, coaches, and male teachers can be open and reflective about their inner experience as they navigate everyday life stress, they learn reflective and emotional skills that benefit us all.

Here are a few additional suggestions for you to consider as you reach out to your son in ways that you likely never experienced as a boy:

Maintain a Constructive Co-parenting Relationship With your Son's Mother

No matter how tempting it may become, never speak ill of your former wife in front of your son. Remember that just as you are essential to your son's healthy development, so is his mom. For your son to mature into a healthy man, he needs you to demonstrate how to respect his mom. Side-step the temptation to become **Disneyland Dad** who parachutes in very occasionally for special treats. Work with his mother on a day-to-day basis to share the parenting load, including mundane duties such as driving him to sports or music lessons, going to parent-teacher conferences, supporting your son's school, health, and recreational needs. Follow through on your agreements so that your son will maintain a sense of security during this time of transition.

Listen to Your Boy

Hear what he has to say. Listen to how he and his friends talk about people, especially females. Ask him if he's ever seen abusive behaviour in his friends. Is he worried about any of his friends who are being hurt in their relationships? Are any of his friends hurting anyone else? Be aware that when we become overly involved in our own challenging life realities, it can be difficult to see our sons as separate people, and really hear their unique ways of perceiving their struggles. Be patient and let him tell his story his way.

Open up Conversations About Things That Matter

Most boys will never approach their fathers and ask for guidance about how to treat people, especially females. But that doesn't mean they don't need it. As a 6 year old, your son is tender and just beginning to develop his emotional vocabulary. He hasn't been shaped by our culture's harsh messages about how boys and men are to behave. He is probably freer now to express his emotions authentically than he will be much later.

Just hanging out with a young son sets a tone for relationship and comfort in each other's presence. While driving in the car, you might inquire about your son's response to another person: "You seemed annoyed with Jake when you made that face. Were you?" Try playing a video game, watching television, or listening to his music with him. If you see or hear things that illustrate disrespect toward others, tell him what you think. Never hesitate to let him know you don't approve of sports figures or celebrities who demean people, or of jokes, video games and song lyrics that do the same.

Be There For Your Son

Strive to be consistently on time when you visit or spend time with your son. Remember that his mother needs time to find her way too and will become stressed when you are late or absent.

Nothing can replace the time you will spend just hanging out and being with your boy. It's like an invisible connective bond that becomes strengthened when you enjoy space and time together. Remember that the time doesn't have to be spent in activity. Boys will probably not say this directly—but they want and need the presence of fathers and significant males around them, even if few words are exchanged.

Become curious about what makes him tick. Take time to linger with him as you pay attention to the mundane details of his life. Check in with yourself, and him later, to see if you can answer the following questions about your son:

- With whom does he spend his time with and whom does he avoid—in his classroom, in the community, and with the extended family?

- What does he absolutely love to do with his free time?

- What annoys him or causes him to become overly stressed?

- What are his likes and dislikes about schooling?

- If he is older, who does he consider to be his best friends?

- What are his favourite comic book heroes? television shows? types of toy? music? pizza? cereal?

- What would he like more of from you?

Teach by Example

Fathers, coaches and men who spend time with boys will have the greatest impact when they *walk the talk*. Your son will learn what mutual respect means by observing how you treat others. Be aware that your son is observing you when you're driving in traffic, talking with customer service reps, with food servers in restaurants, and with your family around the dinner table. Keep in mind that your boy is like a sponge watching and listening to what you say and do and will take his cues from you—both good and bad.

Learning to become a contributing member of society takes time, opportunity, and patience. We all learn to live fully not by ourselves, but through relationships with others.

Be Mindful of How You Respond to Stress

Be aware of how you behave when you are stressed and how you may express your own frustrations or anger.

You might recall during the *Boy Smarts* presentation that I suggested while women typically express their frustrations associated with a difficult day immediately upon arriving home, and perhaps request a hug to make them feel better, men in similar circumstances tend to act stoic or angry. People laugh when I challenge fathers and male mentors to try saying something more honest, something like, "Hello everyone! I'm here and I'm feeling vulnerable. I need a hug. I want to tell you all about my upset."

But for men who did not receive constructive coaching from their own fathers, identifying their own strong emotions and naming them can be hard. Practise checking in with yourself and acknowledging your stress level before you come in contact with your son. At the very least, seek to summarize your emotional state in a matter-of-fact way, an easy one being to identify a number between 1 to 10, with the number 10 meaning that you are highly stressed. Take the time to tell your boy about your stress level and let him know about what you plan to manage this stress, whether something as simple as taking deep breaths, talking about the problem, going for a walk, or working out at the gym.

Teach Stress Management

As humans, we rely on our stress response systems to keep ourselves as safe from as many kinds of danger as possible. Your son's brain is constantly monitoring his environment for potential threats or needs for resources. During the early years parents serve as primary stress regulators, and as children mature, they test the stress template we have provided with our guidance and support. They still need our help—and will continue to well into the teen years—to cope with stress and anger without turning to violence.

Knowing that empathy originates in the family, take the time to teach your son ways to express and manage his stress so that he learns to trust his own stress regulator. Just as when he was an infant and there was no limit to the comforting you could provide him—responding to crying and stressed babies will not *spoil* them—he still needs your attention to his stress signals so that you can in turn teach him to monitor and regulate his own stress. When he gets overly frustrated or angry, tell him he can **walk it out, talk it out,** or *take time out*, but first listen and let him know by your facial expressions that you appreciate his struggle. Let your son know he can always come to you if he feels like things are getting out of hand. Try to give him examples of what you might say or do in situations that could turn nasty. As you are calm and reasonable rather than reactive with him, he too will learn to become reasonable with others, even when he is triggered by irritation. Know too that children who challenge us in respectful ways will also be more likely to challenge peers when they do something wrong, rather than just doing as they are told by others.

While respecting your son's developmental level, take the time to explain why you might appear frustrated and let him know that everything will be all right, and that you will work things out. Take time to explore with your son the options he has to express his own frustration and anger—and what is out of bounds.

Talk with your son about what it means to treat others with respect. Help him work through problems in his everyday relationships as they arise. Let him know he can talk to you anytime, knowing that you will quietly listen and demonstrate compassion and a solid belief that he will find his way. Use every opportunity to reinforce that verbal and physical violence has absolutely no place in a relationship. Let him know how you define healthy relationships and seek to treat people in a way that your son can admire. Be honest with him when you have messed up, knowing that by showing him how to admit mistakes and express humility, your son with learn to do the same.

Seek to Be at the Top of Your Parenting Game

Just as you likely desire the best equipment for the activities you enjoy, equip yourself with the best parenting, disciplining, motivation, and communication skills you can find. Enroll in a weekend or weeknight parenting event or course. Read books. Listen to tapes. Join a support group. If you are able, hire a parenting coach to hold you accountable and help you to be the best dad you can be.

While there is no fixed formula for a father to develop a stronger bond with a son, especially after a divorce, I know that it begins with the sincere desire to be a better dad, followed by positive actions. You will no doubt experience ups and downs along the way, as your father did and his father did before him, but you are venturing down a different path than these men. As you find the courage to reveal your own hopes, disappointments, and struggles, and talk with your son about relationships, you will teach your son that strong men are those who are capable of expressing and managing strong emotions in constructive ways.

As you take regular time to be with your son, he will relax more, and increasing opportunities for the two of you to play together will arise. Allow yourself to be reminded of the times you have managed your own stress in positive ways, perhaps by escaping outdoors away from your parent's fighting. This memory could inspire you to take your son to the beach, looking for rocks or shells, building sand castles without any concern that the waves might come wash them away in the next moment. Positive parenting is less about knowing exactly what to do or how to be, more about finding ways to be in loving presence with your child, open to what the moment—this moment—brings the two of you.

PARENTS, BOYS, & THE CULTURE OF SCHOOLS

• • • • • • • • •

OVER the past several years, I have noticed a swelling need among parents to better understand boys' struggles at school. In my office, on the speaker circuit, and through the website, thousands of parents have emailed their concerns and questions about schooling:

Should kindergarten entry be delayed for boys?

Why are some teachers so quick to raise the ADHD flag before more fully discussing with parents their perspectives about what truly motivates their son's behaviour?

How can classroom learning become more physically and visually engaging, more relevant, and more responsive to the varied needs of boys?

When the going gets tough, why do schools often jump to expedient solutions such as *Zero Tolerance*, school suspensions, and single-gendered classrooms, rather than generate less generic, more nuanced responses to boys' needs?

Why is recess withheld from boys as a punishment when the boys who struggle the most in the classroom need to get outside and release their pent up energy the most?

How can teachers expand and update traditional notions of literacy—academic book learning—to fit the electronic age?

How can teachers encourage the language of caring among boys while honouring their drive for competition?

How can teachers respond more positively to the real needs and fears that may underlie a boy's mask of anger?

9   Should We Delay Kindergarten Entry for Boys?

THE beginning of a school career presents a time of transition often filled with positive anticipation as well as some trepidation. We want our boys to get started on the right track and have a good experience as we launch them from home to school. Some parents wonder whether starting school at the typical age could be too soon.

The following article explores what factors a parents might weigh in considering whether to delay kindergarten entry for a boy.

Should boys start kindergarten later than girls?

Dear Barry,

My son's birthday is in December and I am struggling over whether to start him this upcoming September or delay his entry another year to when he is 6 years old. He is bright, energetic, and mildly interested in reading, but when I watch him play with other kids his age, he seems much more immature. I worry that if he is not ready for kindergarten that he will struggle needlessly.

When I check with my friends, I get mixed reviews. My coworker started her son at age 5 and he is doing fine. He didn't know how to read at first, but slowly warmed up to the idea in his own time. My nextdoor neighbour, who had the opposite experience with her November birthday son, is urging me to hold my son back. She believes that kindergarten is now what First-Grade used to be and that her son's active imagination got stuck behind a desk. I'd appreciate your insight.

Colette

Dear Colette,

At this time of year some parents are starting to worry about whether or not to delay kindergarten for active sons who have so far shown little interest in sitting still and reading. The differing viewpoints expressed by your friends are echoed in parenting blogs, research, and also in the media. The proclamation in the *National Post* in March 2001 that "Boys should start kindergarten a year later than girls to compensate for their slower development rate", caused many parents to take a second look at their son's school–readiness. It's not surprising that parents who read American statistics that seventeen percent of boys are held back at some point in their school career, as compared to only ten percent of girls, are concerned that their sons who like to move around and make noise may not be prepared to sit down and focus on classroom learning tasks. When they have sons whose birthday is in the autumn or early winter, parents may worry that most of their son's classmates will be older and more developed. Above all, parents worry that a negative kindergarten experience will turn their son off schooling from the get–go. Naturally, parents want to make the best decision, one that will start their boys on the road to achievement, success, and lifelong learning.

The Nature/Nurture Debate: Are the gender differences we often notice innate or learned?

There are, of course, boys who prefer to colour quietly while their sisters play with action hero toys. It is more common, however, for gender differences in styles of play and socializing to show up early in life. Some conscientious parents who ban toy guns, and encourage their sons to play cooperative games of *House*, find that the boys are constructing play guns from *Lego* blocks or sticks in the yard. Parents who avoid buying their daughters *Barbies* and pink, frilly clothes may still find their daughters gravitating toward girly–girly toys. Many parents also notice that their 5 year old girls have more impulse control, more verbal fluency, and greater ability to sit still than boys at a similar age, while boys are often more rough-and-tumble and more aware of spatial relationships. Some researchers assert that gender differences are related to brain differences between boys and girls, while others argue that these gender differences are learned.

Are these differences innate, or are they learned from subtle and not–so–subtle social and environmental cues?

While there is no definitive answer here, some evidence suggests that differing developmental tendencies between boys and girls appear early on and appear to be inborn:

- baby boys are more likely to be irritable than baby girls

- infant girls tend to hold eye contact for a longer period of time

- baby boys are less able to distinguish another baby's cry from background noise

- the typical boy develops clear speech by age 4.5 while girls are more likely to articulate clearly at age 3

We can't ignore the possibility that these tendencies could make parents less likely to keep interacting with a fussy or distracted son, or to spend less time reading to him because he appears to be less attentive and responsive. The interface between biology and culture may lead to different developmental pathways for boys and girls.

As you consider the following scenario, ask yourself whether you are likely to respond differently to your son and daughter:

On a Friday evening after dinner, you are tired, but recharging your batteries as you chat with neighbours in your kitchen. Imagine that your pre–school daughter is sitting at the kitchen table nearby playing quietly while taking in your adult conversation. If your pre–school son is also at the kitchen table, but is making loud clanking noises with *Tonka* trucks, how do you respond to him? If you realize that he is in another room quietly playing with his *Lego*, do you invite him into the room and continue to play in this language–rich social gathering? Or is it just easier to leave him playing alone in the other room—losing out on opportunities to absorb language and social skills by osmosis?

We need to consider how our attitudes toward boys and girls may subtly influence our expectations and their learning experiences at home and at school.

As I have never had the pleasure of teaching kindergarten, I have drawn on the wisdom of three experienced kindergarten teachers to explore the question about school–readiness for boys.

Learning From the Wisdom of Experienced Kindergarten Teachers

Laurie, a longtime kindergarten teacher from Langley, runs a play–based classroom, and is careful not to rush children into academic work. She organizes a balanced day to respond to the varied needs of a range of children and believes that all thinking begins with wonder. Laurie has observed that rambunctious boys who were late to speak thrive in her classroom as much as boys who come to school in September already knowing how to read. Laurie doesn't support delaying entry for boys, but emphasizes that classrooms must be balanced, flexible and respect the needs of all children, wherever their readiness. She believes that stressful kindergarten environments which accentuate deskwork, obedience, and please-the-teacher rote memory activities tend to inhibit a child's growth and development. She is critical of the practice of offering worksheets, flashcards, or what she candidly refers to as assembly–line learning at any age. Understanding that brains grow on their own timetable, Laurie advocates different instruction for different children. She even suggests that we should, generally speaking, make Grades 1 to 12 more like kindergarten—that is, more hands-on, more socially engaging, and more inquiry-based. Children in Laurie's classroom playfully create stories, castles, and paintings with one another, developing and refining their abilities to think creatively and work collaboratively, work/play which leads them, in turn, to imagine new ideas and new projects. Laurie argues that inquiry–based learning prepares children for today's fast-changing society, where people must continually develop innovative solutions to unexpected problems and situations that crop up.

When parents are trying to determine whether it is the right time to send their son to kindergarten, Laurie acknowledges that the child's readiness is a factor. Most important, however, is what attitude the school staff hold toward boys, especially boys who are rambunctious. She knows that attentiveness is closely linked to positive emotional cueing.

- Is a child's natural curiosity encouraged without pressure on the child to perform?

- Are students expected to sit still and be quiet most of the time?

- Is the classroom organized so that there is ample opportunity for movement and hands-on exploration that engage all of a child's senses?

- Is there ample opportunity for high–interest repetition and practice that holds children's attention?

- Do boisterous boys rattle the teacher or others in the school?

- When a young boy hits another child or behaves inappropriately, is he exiled to the time-out area or even suspended, or is he supported and guided so that he can maintain self-respect while he learns how to get along respectfully with others?

Another experienced kindergarten teacher from Vancouver, Mandeep, offered a different perspective: "Pushing a boy into a learning environment that he isn't sufficiently equipped for can ultimately result in poor academic performance and unnecessary emotional stress." She points to an American study of kindergarten teachers who reported that forty-eight percent of incoming children have difficulty handling the demands of school.

Her twenty plus years of experience have taught her that some boys are just not ready for kindergarten, and readily acknowledges that today's kindergarten is much more advanced and complex than the kindergarten which parents may have once attended. She believes that when children are old enough to go to kindergarten but are not developmentally ready to succeed, parents ought to exercise their option to delay entry. "Giving some boys an extra year to engage in productive pre–school learning activities just makes sense in view of the research suggesting that the late–bloomers tend to lag behind their classmates."

Mandeep is critical of research findings that most differences related to age and gender seem to disappear by the Third-Grade. She argues that the stories of immature boys are lost in the research data, overlooked in studies of broad achievement statistics that do not consider specific subgroups of children, especially those slower-to-develop boys. She is concerned that in British Columbia, government education documents such as the *BC Early Learning Framework* or the *BC Full Day Kindergarten Program Guide* ignore the issue of kindergarten–readiness for slower–to–develop boys by not even addressing them as a subgroup in their discussion; she points to her school district achievement data indicating boys are more likely to be identified with a learning disability or a behaviour problem than girls. Pointing out that there is relatively little research that looks at academic achievement by gender or by delayed entry to kindergarten, Mandeep speculates that the high rates of ADHD–diagnosis in boys may be related to the different patterns of maturation for boys and girls.

Mandeep also remarks, by the way, that school economic markers are more significant than gender in children's school success, and that children living in poverty are more likely to benefit from earlier entry to kindergarten where they may find increased learning opportunities. She also stresses that while studies indicate socio–economic status to be the strongest predictor of academic success, this need not be the case, adding, "Poverty should not automatically mean academic trouble. What counts is what poverty means to a particular family in a particular circumstance. A family may be poor economically, but live in a home abundantly rich with literature, creativity, and loving exploration."

Mandeep does offer concerned parents some food for thought: "If a boy's first exposure to a formal school setting results in a steady struggle for him to keep up, that impression may stay with him and negatively impact his confidence and future performance throughout his school career." She encourages parents to look beyond achievement data and government documents to consider their son's readiness and unique needs. She concludes that parents should not shy away from delaying entry to kindergarten if this decision seems warranted.

Gary, a kindergarten teacher from Toronto, suggests that parents set up a time to meet with their child's prospective teacher to gather information about the kindergarten environment in their neighbourhood. While many parents begin this process early in the year, Gary suggests that June is not too late to speak with the teacher, to observe the classroom atmosphere, and to consider whether the teacher's teaching style and the overall classroom atmosphere will be a good fit for their son.

Gary says that parents should not assume that boys born later in the year should automatically be considered for delayed entry. Instead parents should draw on the input of pre-school teachers and others who are familiar with their son and understand his needs. "Some boys born later in the school year really benefit from a delayed entry, but only when they spend that year engaging in wide–ranging learning experiences," says Gary. "Staying home and watching television is not wide–ranging enough."

Gary also points out that while the average child can learn to decode words at about age 6, it is normal for children to learn this skill as early as age 4 and as late as age 7, and that the same kind of age range applies to learning to draw, write letters and numbers, count, speak articulately, and follow multiple directions. Parents who learn that some children entering their son's kindergarten already know how to read need not get alarmed. He advises parents to resist the urge to get a head start with flash card *bootcamp* or early reading lessons. Any time spent drilling and pushing academic learning could be more productively spent sharing the silly antics of a character in a read-aloud story, building, digging, creating a project, or visiting the local library. Gary suggests that when parents instill a love of literacy and numeracy—numbers and math concepts—in a relaxed and loving atmosphere, in time all children become eager for new language experiences. He understands that excessive stress releases stress chemicals in the brain that stop learning. "Children will learn to read when they are developmentally ready," asserts Gary. "I'd prefer that children have staggered entry to kindergarten and enter on their fifth birthday, whenever it falls in the year, and that they move along to Grade 1 when they are ready, allowing for those who are developmentally ready to begin earlier and those who are not to have more time without any attached stigma."

Having observed parents—especially fathers—to be more uncomfortable with a shy and reluctant boy at the classroom door than a shy and reluctant girl, Gary also encourages parents to be more accepting of boys who are shy and hang back at their parent's side. He says that shyness ought not be equated with readiness, and that we may be harming boys when we push them to discount their feelings and experiences. While some more sensitive boys may be more reluctant to begin kindergarten, Gary believes that teachers who are familiar with differing needs of children will work with parents and their sensitive sons to create a respectful and smooth transition. He confirms the guidance I provide in *Boy Smarts*: Schools can be a safe haven where academic practices and classroom strategies can provide emotional comfort while they also foster joyful experimentation. When fun and spontaneity are scrubbed from the classroom and replaced with conformity and rigidity, students of all ages disengage—their inquiring minds doze off.

From these three insightful and experienced kindergarten teachers, we learn that readiness is multifaceted. In part, it depends on the child; in part, it depends on the flexibility of the classroom and sensitivity of the teacher. While the perspectives of these teachers differ, they all agree that children who are exposed early on to a rich variety of interactive experiences will be better prepared for kindergarten. Laurie, Mandeep, and Gary each suggest home–based readiness activities to encourage your son's growth and development.

Teacher-Tested Ideas on Encouraging a Love of Learning

1. Whether it becomes a bedtime or early morning ritual, read to your son every day. Children who have been joyfully read to on a regular basis benefit from parental interactions, as well as the exposure to literature.

2. Join your public library and make weekly trips, appreciating that over time your son will appreciate its offerings.

3. Do jigsaw puzzles. Children learn to look at shapes and see where pieces fit, just as they learn to recognize words and numbers by their shape.

4. Arrange building toys in a specific pattern and then challenge your son to copy your pattern, thus increasing opportunities for math logic and reasoning. Invite your son to create a pattern and challenge you to copy it also.

5. To encourage the love of language, sing songs that follow a pattern… for example: *"The cat came back"* or *"I know an old lady who swallowed a fly."*

6. Play memory or detective games with your child. Place items on the kitchen table and allow your son to look for 30 or so seconds, and then get him to turn his back while you remove one item. Can he identify which one?

7. Keep a couple of small books in your car so if you are stuck somewhere you always have the opportunity to enjoy a story.

8. If you want your son to become comfortable with literacy and numeracy, it is important that he observe and believe that reading, writing, and mathematical reasoning are relevant and important to you.

9. Whether you are building something outside or cooking in the kitchen, read the instructions aloud and talk to your son about what you are reading. Take time to estimate then measure together.

10. When driving, point out familiar traffic signs and signs on stores and soon your child will be reading them too. Help him to develop his logic by becoming aware of how the sun helps to determine the direction you are travelling in.

11. If you suspect that your son isn't socially ready for the classroom, provide him with more opportunities to interact with other children in play–based environments.

12. Remember that if you are anxious about your son's readiness, then he will pick up on your anxiety. Consider that most adults you know, whenever they were born and whenever they started school, have in fact learned to read and balance their chequebooks.

Appreciating the Big Picture

Although there are many skills and attitudes considered important for early school success, there is no clearly defined set of behaviours required for a child to enter kindergarten. In fact, the sole entry requirement for kindergarten in British Columbia is chronological age: children are eligible for kindergarten in the calendar year they turn 5 years old.

Parents know that children all mature at different rates. For parents reading this, I believe that your deep love, commitment and understanding of your own boy will allow you to know what's best. If you believe your son is ready, trust and follow your wisdom. If you have nagging doubts, or if you have received feedback from your son's caregiver or pre-school teacher that he may be not ready to begin kindergarten, carefully consider that advice as well.

Trust that you are the best person to determine the best path for your son.

Whether you decide to delay your son's entry to kindergarten or get him started this September, the most important thing is that he engages in active, enjoyable and stimulating learning activities with other people.

James Heckman, Nobel Laureate in Economic Sciences, said, "Early learning begets later learning and early success breeds later success."

Children have compelling common sense, accessibility, honesty, and a complete lack of pretense. They are born ready to learn. The most valuable gift we can give our children is to cultivate and encourage this innate love of learning.

And remember, as the first kindergarten teacher noted, real learning at any age is more like play than it is like work.

10   How Can I Get My Boy to Read?

A common parent lament is that their son is not interested in reading. Expanding our notion of what reading entails and the kind of reading that boys are inclined toward helps us stay encouraged and creative in inviting a boy's participation in developing his reading skills. This chapter explores the multiple ways that literacies develop and highlights the varied ways we can encourage boys to develop their love of reading.

The following article explores what factors parents might weigh in considering whether to delay kindergarten entry for a boy.

Expanding Our Notions of What Reading Entails

Dear Barry,

My son dislikes reading. He loathes to open his Grade 5 novel and later answer the comprehension questions about what happened in the book. He says he'd rather clean his room than answer the questions. I know that he is smart and interested in a lot of things—just not interested in reading novels.

Is this typical for boys?

Ruth

Dear Ruth,

Yes, it is typical that many parents experience frustration that their sons don't read more. Deeply ingrained in our experience of schooling is the notion that reading a novel provides educational sustenance. But is it really that straightforward—especially in our rapidly changing, technologically complex and highly visual society?

It is often typical for boys his age to resist certain forms of literacy. Responsive education understands his lack of enthusiasm and promotes positive reading experiences through literacies he can enjoy.

Indeed, a love of reading has even been shown to be more important for children's academic success than their family's economic background. According to research carried out by the **Organization for Economic Co-operation and Development,** school success is more determined by the extent children read for pleasure in their spare time than their degree of affluence; especially reading forms of literacy they enjoy—comics, magazines, websites, newspapers, games, etc. Encouraging all boys to read for pleasure is essential.

Boys indeed read—but what? The truth is that many boys read widely, just not the books they are sometimes asked to read. Because most lukewarm readers prefer nonfiction it is vitally important that we expand our notion of traditional literacy to include multiple literacies; visual and technological literacy, for example, as well as literacy with forms from the performing arts such as storytelling, music, and video.

In fact, **The United Nations** recently declared, "…that a renewed and expanded vision of literacy is essential for success…that it embraces a wide range of dimensions of personal and social life and development—and that is a lifelong learning process."

Tapping Into Boys' Interests

We can attract boys to reading for pleasure by tapping into their interests and by drawing on a diverse range of texts—for example, technological and media literacies such as text–messaging, decoding of online gaming rules and music lyrics, reading of cartoons, writing of graffiti, blogging, **YouTube**, drawing and even doodling.

Depending on your experience and comfort with the Internet and other digital communication technologies, you might also consider exploring with your son creative ways of reading and communicating online to capitalize on his interests and strengths. If you are in the common situation of knowing less than your son about the computer, let him teach you and share what he knows. Despite the apprehension that the Internet may be rewiring the human brain to be less able to focus—more on this later in the chapter *Hooked on Video Games*—, the Internet offers a world of information and reading opportunities at your son's fingertips that can broaden his learning experiences as he accesses new and creative media, online comic books, *anime* music videos, or even social networking. Most teachers and employers acknowledge that academic and work success in the future will require familiarity and competence with digital media. At the click of a mouse, your son can find advice and information from experts; *Wikipedia*, for instance, is a free encyclopedia built collaboratively to connect the world's knowledge, and can provide a good window into an area of interest.

I know that the Internet presents information that is not always age-appropriate for children, and can even be dangerous; therefore parental controls and/or parental supervision are usually warranted. Along with the skimming, scanning, and evaluation skills many of us learned as children, reading online often requires interaction and special reading strategies. As they navigate multiple links on a webpage, readers who have a clear purpose must learn to quickly evaluate the relevance and quality of sources, and follow a thread strategically, if they are to avoid wandering far away from their original intention.

And your son?—let him know that you believe he is smart and that you understand he is a proficient reader despite his reluctance to read his school novel. Keep your involvement with his home reading assignment positive and encouraging. Avoid forcing him to read.

Find an opportunity to check in with his teacher to glean an understanding of how she or he views multiple literacies and the place of humour and fun to inspire motivation and the love of reading. Explain your son's needs to the teacher.

Boy Smarts offers teachers and parents ten practical guidelines to turn boys onto reading. Teachers everywhere report success when they draw on a wide range of literacy experiences that are fun and socially engaging.

Ten Guidelines From Boy Smarts to Get Boys Reading

1. Teach Multiple Literacies

2. Reach Out to Reluctance

3. Avoid Misreading Violence

4. Bring the Outside In

5. Get Boys Hooked on Books through Humour

6. Offer Show Time

7. Employ Writing Templates

8. Write Less to Get More

9. Value Quiet and Social Reading

10. Become Literate about Adversity

11 What if Your Boy Is Being Bullied?

PARENTS know that they need to teach their children effective skills to respond to unexpected challenges such as bullying in responsible ways. How do we help equip our children to defend themselves against bullying and to seek help when things go too far? It can be difficult for adults to know when to step forward and when to step back, and how to provide children with the chance to learn, test, and practise relational and assertiveness skills. We know that it is important to actively discern the difference between helping and hindering. Given that boys who are sensitive are often at increased risk for being bullied, the following parent email poignantly draws into question how a parent might support a son who is being bullied and is reluctant to speak up.

Boys Need Adult Help to Halt the Cycle of Bullying

Dear Barry,

Last week I learned that a boy reputed to be a bully is in my son's class this year. My boy is 11 years old and is on the shy side. He has those *SpidermanSenses* you talk about at your workshops. He's got friends and does well in school but he's really upset and asked to be moved to another school. He won't tell me who the bully is or even talk about him but I think it might be the boy who picked on him at lunchtime last year and called him gay. Advice?

Cheryl

Dear Cheryl,

We can all appreciate that when toddlers fight over toys and use physical aggression to get their way it is because their verbal skills are not yet highly developed and hitting and grabbing things are ways to communicate their wants and needs. By elementary school it is reasonable to expect that children will grow out of these aggressive tendencies, but not for all children.

Schoolyard bullying is insidious, and can harm boys' potential for learning, expression, and sense of social belonging.

Research shows bullying can have devastating effects: reluctance to attend school; fearfulness or unusual anxiety; sleep disturbance and nightmares; vague physical complaints—headaches, stomachaches; unexplained loss of belongings. It's not surprising that the fear and anxiety of those who are bullied can hinder learning.

Toronto's Board of Education found that one in five children are bullied regularly, often on school grounds. They also discovered that since teachers are aware of only a small percentage of bullying incidents, intervention is difficult.

Even when there is caring, open and effective communication at home, most boys feel reluctant to talk about their troubles. While many fear getting into deeper troubles with the bully, boys who are sensitive and have *Spiderman Senses* especially tend to blame themselves.

The *Boy-Code* teaches boys to be strong and independent—to avoid the social stigma of being labelled a *fag* or *homo.* The word *gay* is loaded with negative power in schoolyard politics.

To prove his masculinity, your son may feel compelled to maintain silence and go it alone.

Anti-Bullying Interventions in Schools

Fortunately many caring and vigilant school staff will understand that they can help to ensure safe and harassment-free learning. They may even have a strategic and effective bully response plan that engages everyone—students, parents, teachers, and the community.

Successful school intervention typically has three components: supporting and protecting those who are bullied; developing consistent, meaningful consequences for the child who bullied; and teaching all students to become caring bystanders who feel empowered to speak against any form of bullying.

Research shows that a range of integrated activities works best. These might include a *Bystander Hero* or *Anti-Bullying* day, an anonymous survey or drop-box to identify trouble spots, daily classroom discussions and role-playing skits before recess and lunch about how respond to bullying, and buddy programs that pair older and younger children.

Schools that develop ongoing peacemaking programs maintain a positive and vigilant focus to stop bullying in its tracks. Research shows that sensitizing the whole school community to bullying issues also helps reduce the subtler forms of bullying that are difficult for playground supervisors to spot.

On a practical level, it is also critical to have adequate supervision of potential areas of risk such as playgrounds, hallways, washrooms, changerooms, secluded areas, school perimeters, trips to and from school, school busses, and Internet use.

Meanwhile, your most pressing task is to respond empathically when your son is reluctant to talk. Here are several suggestions:

1. Listen as he describes his struggle without interruption or advice.

2. Let him know that bullying is NOT okay and you will help him find a solution.

3. Teach him that it's okay to talk about his emotions.

4. Ensure he understands what bullying is—where friendly and good-natured teasing stops and taunting and bullying begin.

5. Share your wisdom while focussing on your boy's resilience, strengths, and positive self-thoughts.

As a caring adult, you may find yourself wanting to fix his situation, but since you cannot always be beside him, that's not always possible—nor productive. As he learns to weather this relational storm, he will most likely becoming stronger in the process. Your job is to continue to listen, maintain open lines of communication, and explore coping strategies with him. Through discussion and role-playing at home and at school, he will acquire action skills that will help him feel more confident when a bully confronts him.

Help your son avoid situations or behaviours that expose him to bullying. If you know that bullying occurs on the way to or from a particular part of the school playground at lunch, find an alternate route and arrange for an older child companion. Be sure he knows where to go for help when he is on route home.

While it is important to help your son to develop skills of self-protection and assertiveness, remember that all children need adult help—the bully, the bullied, and the bystander. Parents and teachers must take bullying seriously and work together to halt the bullying cycle.

12   Freeing Boys from Anxiety

WHY do some boys in high school become moody, irritable, and prone to angry outbursts? This article looks at the hostility in hallways that some boys can bring home, especially boys who are sensitive and prone to anxiety. In my response to a worried parent, I provide suggestions about how we can help mentor a boy's passage to manhood by openly discussing worry and anxiety. In the process we may be able to offer ideas that can help boys cope with the inevitable stresses of maturation in our culture.

Are a boy's explosive outbursts—often saved for parents at home—just a passing hormonal phase or a sign of something more?

Dear Barry,

Recently, our 13 year old son slammed his bedroom door shouting at me "Leave me alone!" I listened to him complain about school and how everybody was a jerk. In the privacy of his room he used strong language that isn't usually spoken in our home. I know that the past four months of starting Grade 8 have been difficult for him, but where did all his frustration and anger come from?

Thankfully, over the recent Christmas break he settled back to the boy that we usually see—quiet, gentle and reasonably happy. We have a good family life and we are close. But I'd sure love to know what happened last fall at school. Why did he become so reactive and irritable? What triggered his anger?

You need to know that Mark has mostly been a shy and quiet boy. Intense anger is uncommon for him. Kindergarten was a difficult transition, with separation tears, but he eventually settled in and did well throughout his elementary years. His classroom teachers would often comment about his quiet nature, mentioning that he rarely offered ideas in class without prompt.

For a couple of years he seemed to enjoy *Cubs,* but he stopped going when the leader left and the new leader provided more time to play floor-hockey. Much like my husband, our younger son loved playing floor-hockey, but Mark would no longer have anything to do with it. I guess he's more shy like me. It also worries me that more recently he has become obsessed with bulking up in our basement.

Should I contact his teachers to talk about his angry outbursts at home if they come back? We have been cautious to not over-stress Mark, knowing that he does better with a more structured and routine family life. I wonder if he needs anger management? At times I feel helpless with him. Maybe I need the counselling? What can my husband and I do to support him?

Suzanne

Dear Suzanne,

We all know that adolescence can especially be a stressful time for boys, as the pressures and expectations increase at home, at school, and in their social lives. When you saw Mark slam his bedroom door, shouting, "Leave me alone!," you must have found it hard to discern whether he is simply frustrated with normal life pressures, or whether he is wrestling with deeper concerns such as anxiety or depression.

Many parents have discovered that in the loving safety of their home, teenage torment seeps out—or explodes!—as irritability and anger. When males consistently present this way, counsellors and medical professionals often suspect underlying depression; however, given your son's positive response to family time over the holidays, I hesitate to suggest a problem with depression. Your comments about Mark's approach to life indicate that he has a sensitive nature and may be prone to anxiety. Boys who are sensitive have *Spiderman Senses.*

He likely needs additional support to make sense of his inner turbulence so that he can acquire coping skills to meet the demands of school life, and beyond. While many teenage boys are embarrassed by their nervousness and hide their true feeling through a stoic mask of what they believe should be presented, Mark, like many boys, is at risk of internalizing his struggle—believing that he is a screw-up—and thus developing a serious problem with anxiety.

Sometimes parents and teachers can overlook a boy's cry for help, writing it off as *boys will be boys.* As we recall our own adolescent angst, we might also be inclined to presume that Mark will somehow get through it as many of us did, but we would all be wise to acknowledge that we never experienced the age as Mark experiences it. Youth today have much greater exposure to disturbing information, over-stimulation, increased expectations, and accelerated rate of change than we experienced. Boys who are sensitive can pulsate with anxiety in a harsh world where *Rambo* rules.

In *Boy Smarts*, I show how parents and teachers must keep in mind that despite a boy's veneer of aloofness, boys can and do worry about many things. They may worry about their changing bodies, and about whether their muscles—especially their penis—are big enough. They may worry about how to respond to an offer of marijuana, which some youth argue is soon to become legal anyway. They may worry about receiving homophobic taunts such as *fagboy,* or racist taunts, such as *raghead* if they belong to a non-dominant ethno-cultural tradition. They may worry about achievement at school or about their parents breaking up.

Ultimately they worry about not fitting in.

Many Boys Tend to Internalize Stress

Note that a boy's anxieties over such matters are not particularly obvious. Today's macho culture seems pumped on steroids. While girls are encouraged to relieve their stress by sharing their problems with others, boys are ashamed to disclose and commonly internalize their stress. They are taught to turn their uncomfortable feelings into anger—which we all know contributes to the number of men felled by accidents, suicides, and heart attacks. The male ritual of using alcohol and drugs to manage and conceal strong feelings only adds to the damage.

Societal attitudes have fostered a silent crisis among males and boys learn that to reach manhood they must be strong without fail. In a cultural climate that associates masculinity with bravado, lassitude, or the overripe masculinity as seen, for example, on *Lenny vs. Spenny,* boys learn to avoid their feelings and toughen up. They must be strong, controlling—and disconnected.

Emotional weakness must be rejected and even obliterated. It's just not masculine enough.

As early as kindergarten, many boys discover that gender rules are already in place. When boys notice that a particular game is popular among girls, they often forbid the playing of this game. Their inner turmoil may express through stomachaches, bed-wetting, and separation anxiety. Sensitive boys like Mark learn that empathy, caring for others, and listening to their own inner struggle is often not tolerated in our culture, and that survival as males requires anxious vigilance.

Then, fresh from their elementary school cocoon, they jostle for belonging in their new and larger social setting in Grade 8—even casual communication between boys pulsates with verbal brutality aimed to keep everyone in a gender straitjacket:

- Buck up
- Get over it
- Take it like a man
- Get some balls
- Don't be a chicken
- Don't back down
- Don't be a wuss
- What a fag

When adolescent boys look for adult male models, they also see a drive for dominance associated with an idealized muscular body shape—the image of a young man with a well developed chest, arm and shoulder muscles along with a *six-pack* abdomen. Size matters among these young adolescent boys. Mark, who likely believes that it's weak and unmanly to admit feelings of worry and despair, may be compensating through his recent interest in weightlifting. He may have bought into the notion that its easier to acknowledge physical symptoms—a torn muscle for example—than to talk about his nervousness.

Pretending Everything is Cool: The Hidden Costs

This desire to measure up—along with peer pressure, boredom, and adversity—can lead boys to experiment with harmful substances. Many older adolescent boys tell me that they would have benefitted from more talk about addiction issues in Grade 8, when their Grade 5 promise to not use drugs became a distant memory.

The academic success many boys experienced during their intermediate years also becomes a distant memory as they discover among their peers it's no longer so cool to do well in school, where the smart boys are referred to as *suck-ups*.

Not surprisingly, in our classrooms boys also cover their anxieties with a convincing veneer of detachment and isolation. It would be easy to conclude that since these boys look all right, they must be all right. We need, however, to consider that their disconnection is likely a mask for worry and fear.

Eventually, this mask has men believing themselves that they are not susceptible to mental health concerns such as depression or anxiety. Many of the men and adolescent boys I meet in my consulting office describe symptoms of anxiety without realizing they even have any. For the most part they believe that they just have to tough it through and eventually life will get better. At times, the traits associated with traditional masculinity seem beneficial—traits such as being action-oriented, strong and willing to protect those in danger, along with an often helpful ability to compartmentalize and be relatively objective; however, I have consistently observed these males make few connections between their mental health and physical symptoms such as headaches, digestive problems and chronic pain.

Unsupported, anxiety can and does lead to problems with schoolwork, family life, friendships, and general health, and also increases the risk of self-medicating with alcohol or other substances. Undiagnosed, males may also become at risk for depression and suicide. The greatest evidence of male vulnerability is in suicide statistics. Among Canadians of all ages, four of every five suicides are male.

Learning to Talk about Anxiety

It is important that you and especially your husband talk with Mark to discuss how men who flash quickly to irritation or anger often overlook, and thus do not deal with, their anxiety.

Mark needs to learn that worry typically consists of a series of distressing thoughts about possible negative future events and often come in the form of *what if* questions that can sometimes lead to further escalation: "What if I get called on today to give the answer? Why won't those guys just leave me alone? What if the teacher is not beside the changeroom next time? Where can I eat lunch to avoid them? How can I get to my locker and down the hallway before they get there?"

Mark also needs to tell the difference between reasonable anxiety—a test that he didn't study for enough—and the unreasonable—worry that comes from nowhere. Once he can determine his level of anxiety about different events in life he can be mindful of what he says to himself about his worry and make healthier choices to manage anxiety. To open up this discussion with Mark I have compiled a list of examples of typical anxiety as well as a list of *over-the-top* anxiety that is characteristic of an anxiety disorder. If he is open enough, take time to discuss the following list with Mark and have him indicate on a scale of 1 to 10 where he sees himself.

Learning to Talk about Anxiety

Typical Anxiety					Over-the-Top-Anxiety				
1	2	3	4	5	6	7	8	9	10

1. Occasional worry about circumstantial events, such as a test or friendship problem, that may leave you upset

2. Feeling self-consciousness in uncomfortable social situations

3. Random case of "nerves" or sweating over an important event such as talking in front of the class

4. Realistic fear of a threatening object, place or situation

5. Wanting to be sure that you are healthy, safe, and harassment-free

6. Anxiety, sadness or difficulty sleeping immediately following a traumatic event

1. Constant, chronic and unsubstantiated worry that causes significant distress, disturbs your social life and interferes with learning

2. Avoidance of common social situations for fear of being judged, embarrassed or humiliated

3. Repeated, random panic attacks or persistent worry/anticipation of another panic attack and feelings of terror or impending doom

4. Irrational fear or avoidance of an object, place or situation that poses little or no threat of danger

5. Performing uncontrollable, repetitive actions, such as washing your hands repeatedly or checking things over and over

6. Ongoing and recurring nightmares, flashbacks or emotional numbing relating to a traumatic event in your life that occurred

I often find that boys—and lots of men—initially prefer to quantify their feelings with a number scale. Perhaps this liberates them from the question many dislike: "How are you feeling?" In their own time boys then frequently elaborate and expand on their experience. This strategy will also help you both maintain perspective, and hopefully develop different strategies for different kinds of anxiety.

Note that not all boys struggle with anxiety in the same way that Mark does. I recall one 15 year old boy who struggled with making friends and reverberated with anxiety, which he tried to overcome by being loud and forcing himself into people's conversations, much to the disdain of his schoolmates.

Talk with Mark about your own experience with worry and anxiety, as a mother and especially as a father, to help him normalize and better understand the way that unbridled worry can absorb us. You might also discuss with him the different ways that people express anxiety at his school: the girl with perfect make-up; the boy who always shouts out the answer; or, the teacher who turns red when an overly confident youth challenges her in front of the class. Know that as he becomes more proficient at identifying the varied ways that anxiety can present itself, he will become more mindful of his own anxiety and ability to navigate and manage escalating thoughts and emotions.

What is needed is a healthy feeling and expression of anxiety so that anxiety will loosen its grip: feeling the energy of worry, separating out the feelings and thoughts, and most important of all, calmly deciding how to manage life's ups and downs, perhaps with help.

Stress Busters

In addition to helping Mark to talk and find new ways to look at life problems you might also consider exploring with him the varied healthy ways that you and his father manage everyday stress. Here are a couple of stress busters I typically recommend to get you started with this discussion:

Stress Busters

1. Get your body moving. Exercise is a proven stress reliever. When feeling tense, angry, or anxious, turn off the T.V. or computer and get active—bike, run, swim, walk the dog, or any activity, especially outdoor pursuits. Movement helps the brain to process emotions.

2. Be mindful about how you breathe. Take some slow, calming breaths. Close your mouth and breathe in through your nose and exhale out slowly through your mouth. Breathe in slowly to the count of 4, 5, or 6 and slowly out to the count of 8, 9, or 10. Long and slow exhalations really help to get the stress out of the body.

3. Use imagination to take a trip in your mind's eye to a peaceful place where you can relax and have fun. You will need a quiet place to do this exercise. Think of a favourite place you have visited in the past—a special beach, a hiking trail in the woods, or a vacation you enjoyed. Imagine being there again. As you leave your tension behind for a few minutes you will feel calm and relaxed.

4. Listen to relaxing music, read a good book, or even watch an uplifting movie. Notice how your body feels less wound up like a pretzel and more relaxed like a noodle. Do you smile and feel happier inside? Do you feel stronger, maybe refreshed, and even more energetic?

5. Get enough rest and eat healthy food. When we are tired from lack of sleep or not eating properly, it is much harder to face problems.

6. Get away from your worry and do something for other people. Experience has taught me that this helps to take our minds off our own problems and stirs up a good feeling of satisfaction when we make a constructive difference in the life of another.

In your email, I noticed a reference to your younger son as being more like his father, preferring to play floor hockey, and Mark being more like you, shy. While I don't want to read too much into this, Mark may additionally benefit with a frank discussion about genetic predisposition, and how there may be a pattern of heightened anxiety, linking his tendency to worry with your own— if that is in fact true for you—and perhaps to your own father or perhaps your brother, his grandfather and uncle. You may even be able to encourage a male relative that your son admires to discuss his own anxiety openly with Mark so that Mark can further broaden his understanding of the role genetics can play and might just possibly learn new skills to manage his feelings.

Whether with a relative or with someone at home, regular discussions about real emotions in daily life will give Mark permission to have an internal life, approval for the full range of human emotions, and help in developing an emotional vocabulary so that he becomes more confident with managing his own sensitivities.

We can also do this by emphasizing the positives of being a male while also finding ways to assist boys and men in getting the support they need. Part of this is assuring them that we do not consider them less masculine by having a failing or weakness, or by needing to ask for help. It is fear that hamstrings many of us men. Fear that admitting we can't go it alone will trigger outside ridicule. Fear that admitting we need assistance will cause us to feel like less of a man on the inside.

Monitor your son's relationship with stress—his behaviour, thoughts, or feelings—and listen carefully to what he isn't saying as you keep an eye open for increased emotional overloading. If Mark shows signs of excessive stress and is not open to discussing what's going on, be aware that a consultation with a *Registered Clinical Counsellor*, School Counsellor, or mental health professional may help you to explore the matter further. Every school counsellor knows that helping youth manage anxiety is central to their job. Mark may even be open to talking to a counsellor on his own for life coaching, but don't push him into it.

As parents, we all wish we could steer our kids around the inevitable bumps along the path to adulthood. But bumps happen. As you appreciate your son's struggle with life's potholes, and mentor him to learn how to discuss anxiety more openly, maintain your focus on his ability to overcome and fight back against the anxiety—to live a good life. Your belief in his ability to not only cope, but thrive, will provide him a cheerleading team of support—You can do it, Mark!

Finally, remember that helping Mark talk about his inner world and find his own way to balance his emotions is the key. Boys will be open about their feelings when we create safe opportunities for them to do so. They will learn that too much or too little of emotions like worry, frustration, and anger can be a problem. They will become heedful of the negative effects of male rage. But they will also learn that stifling of an emotion, like anger, can also be a problem. They will also learn that an unhealthy inhibition of emotions increases their risk for illness. While Mark may from time to time have outbursts like he did last fall, trust that as his parents you can talk with him and support him to find love and acceptance as he matures to manhood.

When boys like your son Mark learn that emotional courage is the source of real strength in life, for males and for females, we all benefit in ways that we may not have previously imagined.

13   Should I Reward My Son With Cash for Grades?

VERY few of us have not tried the use of external incentives to motivate our boys to perform better in school or in social situations. In our wish to encourage our children, it is easy to get sidetracked and confuse *motivation* with *manipulation*. The following email inquires about rewards to motivate higher academic grades and offers parents insight as they consider the differences between *motivation* and *manipulation* as well as what will really endure in their son's life.

Motivation and Manipulation Are Not the Same

Dear Barry,

Lately, it seems that parent's are doling out cash as a way to *kick-start* their son's motivation to reach for higher grades. Rewards seem to make sense, yet I'm confused. Don't they also create a monster who gives to get? I really don't want to become one of those parents who gives their kids money for making their beds, cleaning their rooms and helping set and clear the table. And I certainly don't want my son to learn that life is more about rewards than results, that working hard is only worth it if you can buy something at the end, or that contributing only matters if you get something in return. But is seems tempting. What do you think?

Sara

Dear Sara,

Parents who use cash to inspire grades at school might be surprised to learn that they just may be impeding their son's potential for real learning. While plenty of parenting books advise against punishment, you'll have to look awfully hard to find books that discourage rewards. At first glance, the offer of "$100 for every A" might sound like a fair and reasonable incentive, positive reinforcement, and even preparation for the real world of work. However, a deeper look will show that temporary compliance for short-term gains is strikingly ineffective at producing lasting changes in school achievement—or life for that matter.

Of course, I do not intend in any way to question our well-founded desires to support and encourage boys or celebrate success. I am concerned instead that faith in the power of money to inspire and sustain student success will backfire. Rewarding good grades with cash may undermine your child's independence, pleasure, and interest. The external motivation of working toward money may also undermine a child's appreciation of the intrinsic pleasures of learning.

"But wait a minute," you might be saying. "It seems so commonsensical. After all don't employers reward achievement to motivate and stimulate ingenuity?" While you might hear the media advocating cash incentives for performance, corporate leaders learned long ago the hidden pitfalls of cash rewards. They are a disguised form of control, seducing employees to focus on the prize instead of the task at hand. They work against cooperation and teamwork, the real engine of ingenuity and productivity. In fact, workplace studies find that incentive-driven employees will not ask for help when they need it, conceal problems so to appear capable, avoid risk-taking, and also shy away from collaborative creativity. Social science research confirms that people who expect to receive a reward do not perform as well as those who expect nothing.

"But isn't money a motivator for kids who want money?" you might wonder. The simple truth is that cash incentives motivate your son to want cash, but is this what you are trying to motivate? Cash simply won't influence your son to perform better unless he already wants to; it also won't help him become genuinely interested in what he is learning. Youth see through the manipulations involved in incentives and sugarcoated control. I'll not forget the clever remark a Grade 10 boy once offered to me: "If they have to bribe me to do it, it must be something I don't want to do."

Rewards and Incentives May Backfire

Countless experiences and discussions with teens have taught me first-hand that adolescent desire for independence is stronger, most of the time, than the desire to please parents and teachers. In our own home I have also noticed that when I leaned one way, our boys tended to lean the other. I believe that the adolescent pursuit of freedom from control will trump the desire for cash almost every time. Remember that attempts to manipulate easily backfire. If good grades can be used to please you, bad grades can be used to provoke you. Just ask a teacher or school principal's adolescent son or daughter!

Rewards can also flip into punishment. Cash for grade depends on satisfying you, and when the going gets tough, your son's focus on the far-off prize may shift to an awareness of being controlled. The frustration associated with the withheld cash then seems like a punishment. And the more desirable the reward, the more demoralizing it is to miss out.

When grades slip and you worry about your son's future, it may be tempting to dangle incentives. Keep reminding yourself, however, that growing up is circuitous not a linear process. Lessons—even the lessons associated with failing if need be—will strengthen and test your son's resources and gradually fosters resiliency.

"So what are the alternatives to cash incentives?" you might ask?

Empower Your Son to Take Responsibility for His Own Grades

Listen to your boy talk about his grades—and provide him with time and space to reflect as he tests out ideas and options. When he comes up with complaints and excuses, you also might be tempted to take the bait, offering advice or clarification here and there. You can be certain that your son is counting on you to play this role. Instead, I recommend that you avoid taking responsibility for his grades and his career at school. Trust that he will ask for advice when he wants it, and when he is ready to receive it.

Ultimately it is your son's choice to improve or not improve grades. Your task is to support his path of learning. You can do this through supportive comments that communicate a deep appreciation for your son's struggle to overcome boredom and inertia, and for any sign that he is assuming responsibility for his own learning. Consider how the following comments reflect empathy, support, and appreciation for your boy exactly where he is:

- "You don't have to be perfect or the best at school."

- "It's okay to make mistakes and learn by doing something over."

- "You don't have to hurry and succeed all at once."

- "Asking for help is a sign of real courage and strength."

- "There are some things that we just have to slog through."

- "I know you could do better if you wanted to. What do you want?"

Rather than bribes or threats, pose a question that shows you trust your son's ability to figure things out: "What do you think we can do to solve this problem?" Of course, this emphasis on your son's strengths and resources rather than his difficulties and undeveloped talents requires a conscious shift in your attention. It also requires care, patience, and the willingness to accept that your son is his own person. While incentives such as treats might motivate your dog to obey, they won't have any lasting effect on stimulating ingenuity and scholarly pursuit in your son. Stay interested in his school activities and achievement, but let the pleasures of success and the frustrations of failure belong to your boy. Have faith. He'll figure it out. Ultimately, your faith in your son and your focus on long-term visions will *pay off* for both of you.

14   Hooked on Video Games!

MANY criticize electronic gaming as a distraction from learning. However, for every opportunity computers offer for wasting time, don't they also offer opportunity to increase the availability and diversity of our knowledge? In addition to the amazing number of free downloadable books available through **Google**, ebooks are now outselling hardcover books at **Amazon**, and the trend is accelerating more each day. In a digitalized world, people across the globe are collaborating in business, education, arts, government policy projects—and, of course, digital role-playing games—in ways unheard of in the past. What are the pros and cons of the video games that hold so many boys in thrall?

What if Your Son Prefers "World of Warcraft" to Eating Dinner?

Dear Barry,

I really enjoyed your presentation about mentoring boys at home and school, but I disagree with your comments about video game use.

As a father of a 12 year old son and as an elementary school teacher for ten years, one of the main beliefs I hold dearly is that the use of video games, the Internet, and even the television should be strongly discouraged, limited, if not banned outright from the house. They can be highly addictive. They also teach values that are contrary to social responsibility. There are many researchers who support my view.

In our home we don't have a television, but very occasionally we take in a local movie or video. While we also don't have any gaming stations, my son has a very old hand-me-down *Gameboy*, which he hasn't touched for a long time. We allow him to play the occasional game on the Internet in our room where we can easily see what he is playing. He certainly knows that he is not allowed games involving violence.

He complains occasionally, but generally he is pretty content, as he fully understands our reasons to limit his screen time. Instead, he is very active physically with martial arts, street hockey, basketball, soccer, and swimming. He bikes everywhere and practises his violin almost everyday.

It's a lot more work for us to keep him stimulated than to have him plugged into a computer, but he is an incredibly well adjusted kid. He gets straight A's without really trying, and we put no pressure on him to succeed whatsoever.

I think the use of video games, the Internet, and other types of electronic-based media are really detrimental to children's language development. It's the primary reason why today's kids think reading sucks! My son was reading the *Iliad* and the *Odyssey* several years ago. My wife read one of the two epic books of poetry to him first. Since he loved it, he then chose to take the second book out the library to read himself.

He is not asymmetrically developed in any way. He's just literate and loves reading.

The human species has been around for about 50,000 years or so without television, *Gameboys, Xbox, Playstation* or the Internet. Don't you think we can live without most of these items—at least without the highly addictive video games?

Simon

Dear Simon,

I know that many thoughtful parents and educators like you, Simon, are concerned about the dangers of emerging technologies, especially the potential addictiveness of video games. I often hear parents worrying aloud about how to manage the time their sons spend playing video games. When we read headlines depicting video games as mind-numbing *Crack* and media articles that compare gamers to strung-out heroin addicts, it's no wonder we worry about the long-range influences these electronic games may have on our boys.

For many the video game alarm sounded in 1999 when the media suggested that violent video games provoked the Columbine school shootings; some analysts even argued that part of the killers' problem might have been desensitization due to their constant exposure to violent imagery in these games.

Recently, we learned that the world's most wired nation—South Korea—has portrayed video games as violence-ridden vehicles after ten people died from playing games in 2005, including one twenty-eight year old man who collapsed in an internet cafe after playing an online game for fifty hours.

You might be interested to know that a very large percentage of the general population plays video games regularly, but the amount of time playing is unrelated to ethnicity, household income level or parent's level of education. Boys greatly outnumber girls as game players; last year's July issue of *Archives of Pediatrics and Adolescent Medicine* reported that eighty percent of all boys and just twenty percent of all girls.

What is a parent or teacher to think? Are we becoming a *play station nation*? Wouldn't youth be better off reading books?

Become Familiar with Gaming Strengths and Drawbacks

Instead of seeing video games as dangerously addictive, many are suggesting now that playing these games can make our kids smarter and adaptive. They argue that video games actually stimulate the brain, that through the wonders of our brain's neuroplasticity, games can actually retune the brain to become more efficient and can even reduce symptoms of ADHD.

Studies also reveal that among the generation of children growing up wired, knowledge gleaned through video game playing can be transferred to other activities, sparking motivation to learn a special skill such as how to create a podcast, direct a **YouTube** video, publish an *anime* site, or hack an *iPhone*.

As we see how youth take to these new technologies, I can't help but wonder what might happen with boys' school engagement and achievement if teachers had the resources to provide similar educational nourishment to inspire such ingenuity. Parents who banish boys to their bedrooms to complete school assignments must wonder why many of these boys are willing to spend hours and months struggling and delaying gratification to get to the next level in an electronic game.

Given that just last week the sales of *Grand Theft Auto IV* surpassed all records for video gaming revenue, with first week sales reaching just over half a billion US dollars, it would seem that the market for video games is here to stay. Thus it only seems sensible, while considering the potential influences of these electronic games, to familiarize ourselves with their strengths as well as their potential drawbacks.

Oddly enough, I have noticed that parents and educators who are critical of video games rarely report playing video games. Not being an avid video gamer myself, for many years I tended to believe the bad press about these games, until I began to really listen to the conflicts between parents and their sons, and especially to what boys had to say about video games. I have learned that most boys who play:

- enjoy the spatial and highly visual challenges presented by video games
- thrive on sorting through hypotheses in order to make sense of the game's environment
- take pleasure in managing a dizzying array of information and options
- appreciate the complex problems they solve to achieve success
- willingly delay gratification for weeks to get to the next level
- attach importance to finding meaning in the game's world, and making decisions that help create order and predictability
- value the tangible results games provide
- understand the line between game violence and violence in life
- welcome the social interactions that gaming provides
- collaborate with others to achieve success

Watch Out for Addiction

But what happens for boys who develop problem usage and even perhaps become addicted to video games?

While there is currently no video game addiction category in the ***Diagnostic and Statistical Manual of Mental Disorders***, and last year's attempt to include it in the manual was rejected for lack of sufficient evidence, there is a small percentage of boys who struggle with controlling their problematic thoughts as well as the amount of time they play. Naturally, we need to look for ways that help them control their game playing, so that the games do not control them.

While most boys are simply relieving everyday stress through playing video games, it is still a good idea to be alert to the warning signs of addiction. If a boy becomes violent when asked to stop playing a game, it may be a strong indication that there's a problem.

There are three hallmark indicators that professionals use to diagnose an addiction:

- a compulsive and physiological craving

- the need for higher doses to obtain the same effect

- distressing and uncomfortable symptoms during withdrawal

If a boy appears to be struggling with any of these symptoms, parents need to consider the degree to which their son's game playing behaviour could be a problem that interferes with his everyday functioning. Over-engagement with video gaming, along with prolonged withdrawal from family, friends, and life in general may mean that you need to seek help.

But parents also need to consider whether the obsessive playing of video games is a problem or a symptom.

Remember too that just as adult addictions may take many forms besides excessive use of substances—too much time spent working or shopping, for example

—video games may not be the main cause of an addiction, but simply the milieu or backdrop where addictive personality tendencies get played out.

It is also worth noting that a parent's perception of a son's video game playing is very subjective. I bet that you rarely find yourself complaining about a boy obsessing with playing a newly learned musical piece or completion of a school project. We need to be cautious in how we judge our boy's gaming world, or we are prone to be reactive and even dismissive.

Many parents may feel overwhelmed by fear if they consider that their son may have deeper emotional problems than the one presented by his game playing; thus they may focus on limiting access to games when their son really needs help for deeper underlying issues—perhaps anxiety, depression or disturbing thoughts and emotions.

More often I have discovered that boys who struggle with traditional classroom book learning, listening to lectures and completing written assignments, seek success through the feeling of competence and intelligence they get by playing video games. When parents over-react by withdrawing all game play, they may be inadvertently pushing their son toward further despair and disconnection.

Meanwhile, I agree with your basic message about taking the time and attention to seek a balanced family life that encompasses varied activities and opportunities within the community. Get outside and bike together, read together, and develop broad sustainable interests.

Learn from Boys About Video Games

I don't necessarily think, however, that we would be better off without video games and up-and-coming technologies. Maybe we need to sit with our boys and learn from them how to play video games. Showing interest in their electronic world will help us connect with our sons, and will also place us in a better position to discuss limits and other sensitive issues about the ideas and cultures presented within games.

In fact, with a bit of good fortune we will mostly come to learn that the new digital technologies are bringing up a new generation who are creators of media rather than just passive consumers; that within these digital environments among peers, boys who create and evaluate media will derive a sense of competence, autonomy, self-determination and connectedness.

Finally, I invite parents and teachers to consider to what degree our homes and schools are disconnected from real-world literacies so revered by boys surfing the edge of technology. What might happen if we embraced boys' interest and level of engagement with video games as well as other opportunities afforded by the internet in our schools?

As knowledge is changing so rapidly, we need to adapt to these changes, seeking balance in our children's world, with digital technology, like sports, music, and literature, another rich area for exploration.

As for video games—I suspect that in ten years time we will discover what my mom told me about my love of rock collecting and go-cart building decades ago when I was a boy:

Moderation is key.

Postscript

The article *Hooked on Video Games* generated a lot of controversial heat while it also attracted plenty of positive support from both parents and teachers. Some hold strong to their beliefs that emerging technologies are harmful for children, while others used the ideas as a springboard for Socratic dialogue with boys, and some wanted to hold on to multiple perspectives: In my view, digital media and technology are unstoppable and we ought to get on board if we are to influence the outcome.

It is clear that the topic is still contentious and worthy of further exploration. From several passionate emails, I have selected two that I believe draw attention to highlight concerns not considered in the original article. One concerns a discussion between a mother and teenage son about digital alarmists. The other is from a parent worried about her son who has witnessed violence. My responses speak to the importance of parents and teachers becoming cautiously optimistic about the new potentials in our wired world.

Beware: Overly Strict Limits on Gaming May Backfire

Dear Barry,

My 16 year old son Amar is trying to convince me that video games are good for him. He has been doing a research project for school and says he discovered that in recent years a drop in violent crime has accompanied increased use of video games. He even suggests that video gaming provides him and others the opportunity to release their pent up anger and rage in harmless ways. He argues that replacing real enemies with virtual ones makes our communities safer. Is this true?

Despite Amar's social awkwardness, he gets good grades and we are basically pleased with his behaviour, except for his incessant arguing with his father about wanting more computer time. Yet, I am encouraged as we debate what he calls the *digital alarmists*. I have to admit that my husband too is a *digital alarmist*. He is exceptionally strict and rigid with video gaming time, and will even pull the plug when Amar's time is up. I feel their tension mounting and find myself between them. I would like to see my son as capable to assess critically the digital world that is so important to him, yet my lack of personal knowledge leaves me wondering if my husband is right: that if we give him an inch our son will take a mile. Any suggestions you have would be greatly appreciated.

Ella

Dear Ella,

Your son is correct when he says that in recent years, along with an increase in video gaming, there has been a decrease in violent crime. However, we are not sure whether gaming releases pent up anger in harmless ways by replacing real enemies with virtual ones, although this hypothesis has a certain appeal.

Generally speaking, I am encouraged whenever I learn about teenage boys asking critical questions about the technologies they use—whether they're critiquing online gaming, the reliability of web information, personal privacy on the Internet, or issues about web-based literacy versus printed texts. High school teachers have also told me that they can draw on students' knowledge of role-playing in the gaming world when they are exploring academic questions about the structure of narrative and character development.

Frequently, I have discovered that open-minded discussions about the pros and cons of video gaming between parents and their teenage sons can often help to mitigate the negative effects of the violence in these games.

While clear limits and restrictions are effective for younger boys, for adolescent boys, lure of the forbidden will likely increase their attraction to violent gaming. I imagine your husband is concerned about your son's social development, but he would be better off spending time cultivating connection with your son in low-key ways rather than imposing sanctions on gaming.

You might be interested to also know that shy and introverted adolescent boys may find interpersonal connections with online gaming or social networking. Discussions with these anxious boys have taught me that online communication and gaming are not just a pale substitute for face-to-face interaction, but provide a sense of real, meaningful social connection.

Are Some Boys at Greater Risk of Aggression Than Others?

Dear Barry,

I understand that moderation is important when it comes to time boys spend playing video games, but I worry about the influence of violent video games on my son specifically. Police removed my son's father from our home several years ago because of his violent outbursts, and my son witnessed several assaults between ages 6 to 9 years old.

Years ago I read a study about the effects of televised violence, and now that my son is 16, I worry about the amount of time he plays *World of Warcraft*. I wonder what this game might be teaching him, and what purpose video gaming could serve in a boy's world.

As a single mom, I also worry that my son is at increased risk to follow his father's path. He has many similar qualities to his father, especially as he gets easily frustrated and prone to outbursts. Yet I also see that he is different, more kind, more social, and more talkative than his father. His teachers report that he is engaged and achieving well at school.

More recently, I have been talking with him about the ideas from your *Hooked on Video Games* article and feel as though we have opened a door of discussion that will be productive.

Still, I lose sleep that he will be damaged by the violence in these games.

Karen

Dear Karen,

It is true that some studies have shown that boys who watch violent television were more aggressive afterwards. Many parents and teachers draw parallels between television violence and video game violence, although, of course, television is passive while video gaming is interactive. Given that evidence also tells us that aggressive children are more likely to be attracted to violent media, I fully appreciate your concern about the amount of time your son spends playing *World of Warcraft*.

Because recent evidence also tells us that the human brain is a social organ and requires human reciprocity and interaction to develop fully, many also wonder how boys will develop empathy from a game such as *World of Warcraft* that appears to focus on violence. For their brains to develop fully, even older boys like your son still need touch, warmth, and presence. These are things that many assume video games do not provide.

Or do they?

I am not certain how much you know about *World of Warcraft*, or even if you have watched your son playing it. Do you know that the game boasts 6.5 million online players worldwide, typically gaming twenty hours per week? Or that thousands can be logged in simultaneously, interacting with players across the globe in a vast virtual fantasy setting full of pitched battles, directly or indirectly influencing the lives of other players' characters? Do you know if your boy has joined a team—called guilds—that tackle game challenges collaboratively? Guilds view their membership as a commitment and expect participation in virtual raids and other joint activities. The ongoing and intense interaction with other players often leads to friendships and personal connections.

In many discussions with boys, I have learned that yes, there is a real risk that some will become obsessed with the struggle to increase their virtual wealth and status in the game—while they earn access to higher game levels and more exciting content. Still others are able to maintain a healthy perspective and enjoy the game's social entertainment value, along with the satisfaction of achieving greater mastery.

More to your question: Witnessing violence in the family—as your son has done—does create increased risk of aggression. Even though studies like *The Role of Media Violence in Violent Behaviour* by Huesmann and Taylor (2006) show that a small percentage—4 to 9%—of violence could be traced or exacerbated by the viewing of violence, I also worry that for some boys, too much virtual aggression could make a bad situation worse. Sadly, experience has taught me that the most vulnerable boys are often those most attracted to violent gaming—that is, boys who have poor attachments to adults.

If you do observe your son lashing out with explosive anger in the real world at any point, you may consider enrolling him in a martial arts course or paying for a personal fitness trainer to help him manage his anger and express it in safe, clean ways.

For now, I note that you have identified your son as well-adjusted with traits that will help him weather any storms as he grows into manhood. Mostly, I am encouraged that both you and his teachers do not report any violent outbursts. I encourage you to take some solace that *World of Warcraft* teaches more than violence. Kindness, sociability, as well as your ability to talk through problems are tremendous protective factors that can overcome the effects of witnessing violence in the early years.

15   Are Boys Spending Enough Time Outdoors?

AT the beginning of the twentieth century, American botantist Luther Burbank wrote: "Every child should have mud pies, grasshoppers, and tad-poles, wild strawberries, acorns, and pine cones, trees to climb and brooks to wade in, sand, snakes, huckleberries, and hornets, and any child who has been deprived of these has been deprived of the best part of his education."

The average North American child spends less than a half hour a day learning from, and delighting in nature.

What are these indoor children missing?

Nature is Our Universal Healer

> **Dear Barry,**
>
> When the weather is good, my 7 year old son wants to play outside, but there is no one on our street for him to play with. During the school year our local elementary school is bursting at the seams with kids, but now they are nowhere to be found. Why aren't more parents getting their kids outside more? Are they afraid the kids will get abducted or injured? Do the kids prefer to stay inside and watch video games and television? While getting my haircut yesterday, I overheard a woman talking about her plans to buy $5000 TV for her youngest boy this summer because *Pokémon* is no good if it's not in HD. Why aren't parents using any extra cash to buy bikes or camping gear? Is this typical? How can we get our boys outside more?
>
> **Saika**

Hi Saika,

Today, I find myself walking on a sunny day in mid-June, walking along a beach trail in British Columbia. The southerly wind keeps the late spring heat at bay and in the distance I notice a kite with a long red tail darting and dancing in the sky. I remember the joy I got from designing, constructing, and flying kites as a boy. As I move closer toward the dancing kite, I soon discover that the ones at play are adults, not kids. Looking further down the beach, I begin to wonder why I'm not seeing more children.

Could they be at their local parks playing *Capture the Flag*, swinging from monkey bars or shooting hoops? Cycling or skating around their neighbourhoods? Testing their entrepreneurial skills with a lemonade stand?

Could they, on this delightful spring day, possibly be inside, glued to a television or electronic screen?

Although I believe that video games and digital entertainment have their uses, I can't help but wonder how kids will refresh and renew this summer without plentiful access to nature and green outdoor spaces.

Of course, it's easy to wax nostalgic about the role nature played in our free-range childhood—the endless hours of unstructured play—digging in the dirt or building forts in backyards; practicing new bicycle tricks on our neighbourhood streets; observing plant life, birds, insects, or animals in community parks.

Unless you were allergy prone, it is likely that your summers afforded freestyle adventure play at its best, with no admission charges, restricted hours of operation, or overly constraining rules of engagement.

I suspect that our own parents wanted us to be safe, but I don't recall my mother scheduling play-dates or driving me around the corner to a friend's house. I also doubt that she was worried about stranger danger and other hazards while I gallivanted across our neighbourhood in search of adventure, friends, and fun.

Ironically, despite many studies demonstrating that violence is actually decreasing in our communities, our fears of risk and danger for our kids have intensified. And the more our kids shy away from spending time in nature, the more they begin to view it as uncontrollable and off-limited wildness, something to be protected from rather than connected with.

It's also sad that educational leaders—perhaps out of fear of litigation—do not challenge our culture's risk aversion in the way that David Bell, **OFSTED's** chief inspector of schools —**The Office for Standards in Education in Britain**—, does. He argues that risk is part of life, and that children need to learn about risk in modulated ways: "One of the best ways to help children to learn about risk is to teach them how to deal with difficult and tricky situations by allowing them to experience them in controlled conditions." After all, how can children, who are part of nature themselves, come to be fully alive if they are not allowed to engage in complexities and challenges outdoors?

Richard Louv, author of *Last Child in the Woods: Saving Our Children from Nature-Deficit Disorder*, and chairman of the **Children & Nature Network,** argues that society is telling kids an unintended message that nature is in the past, that the bogeyman lives in the woods, and that the future is in electronics. He also draws from scientific evidence showing that direct contact with the outdoors promotes healthy physical, cognitive, and emotional, child development.

In the United States, the **House of Representatives** last year overwhelmingly approved a *No Child Left Inside Act* that will promote environmental literacy in the schools. Similarly, the **BBC** reported this past spring on a Scottish government initiative to boost the amount of time that pre-school children spend outdoors, and a push for educators to restore more risk and adventure to their classrooms.

While we need to balance risk and safety considerations along with the integration of electronic media into a boy's world, we also need to find ways to get our children outside more where they can experience the wonders of our natural world beyond a screen—especially in the summer.

The Benefits of Being Outside

Many studies have found that exposure to nature helps promote active and engaged learning for children. Childhood play in nature reduces stress, encourages creative social play, reduces symptoms of attention deficit disorder, and provides a foundation for environmental awareness and responsibility that carries over into adult life. Studies have also demonstrated that childhood play in more natural diversified settings, with uneven ground, trees and shrubs rather than in smooth, built environments also sparks more imaginative and varied play. And of course, with all the talk now of childhood obesity, childhood outdoor play is a fun way for children to keep in shape. **OFSTED** has found that outdoor activity "contributes to personal growth and social awareness" and "to health and fitness and continuing participation in outdoor pursuits" throughout life. Significantly, it also "introduces young people to the environment in a way which develops understanding appreciation, awe, wonder and respect... [and] the need for sustainable use of the world's natural resources."

Social psychologist Francis Kuo, in the *Journal of Environmental Psychology*, highlights the value of any exposure to nature in childrens' emotional and intellectual development, indicating that even the mere "presence of a tree outside the window of a child living in the ghetto improves self-discipline, behaviour, and academic achievement." Indeed, the healing effects of nature extend to us all. Eric Weiner, in *The Geography of Bliss*, reports on a 1984 study by psychologist Roger Ulrich that patients recovering from gallbladder surgery with a natural window view recuperated much faster than those whose rooms overlooked a brick wall.

Nature refreshes the life of the spirit. As Thoreau once said, "In wildness is the preservation of the world."

In the hopes that you and your family will reap some of the many benefits of being in nature, I offer the following suggestions.

Discover Next-door Nature

Sometimes we are blind to the nature we live next door to because we expect nature to be so much wilder and grander—perhaps a place that we travel to on summer vacation or a national park—but to children, your local ravine is a universe. Perhaps you have a ravine behind your home or a little woodsy enclave at the end of the street. Nature flourishes in these small local areas. I recall a recent neighbourhood walk with a boy who noticed a fern poking its way through a paved walkway in search of survival. A little later, as we talked about new opportunities arising from his recent struggles at school, the boy noticed new growth arising from the dead limb of a tree. Without words, nature teaches about nature's cycles and processes, about letting go and regeneration.

Build Walking Into Your Routines

Taking the time to walk slowly, to notice and reflect on what you see around you—trees, plants, animals, rock formations and wildflowers—can be very restorative. Let yourself sense the light summer wind, and the warmth of the sunlight as it filters through a canopy of treetops. Take the invitation nature offers us every day—to slow down, pause, pay attention, and breathe.

When grandparents, relatives, or friends come to visit, begin the visit with a walk through your local area. Notice how this family ritual gently attunes you to nature's rhythms, and to increased awareness of your own rhythms. Walking creates the time and space to talk, or to be silent. Appreciate that for highly kinesthetic boys, walking and simple exposure to natural settings has been shown to reduce symptoms of ADHD, says the ***American Journal of Public Health.***

Cultivate an Interest in Bugs

There is nothing more interesting to a young boy than bugs, worms, or unusual looking insects. Having a natural curiosity, kids learn quickly as they observe an army of ants taking little bits and pieces to build their homes. A honeycomb or a chrysalis' struggle to become a butterfly reveals the wonder of nature. With support, children may come to realize that the world is bigger than they are, and holds many wonders to discover and appreciate.

Go Camping

Camping in a tent and outdoor living for a time can be a great antidote for the consumerism of our society. Setting up a tent, cooking meals, and hiking a rough trail can help kids move directly into present experience while also creating lasting memories. Children can learn about local species of trees, plants, birds, animals, about the fluctuations of weather and temperature, about gathering and splitting wood—with a sharp axe—to prepare for a campfire. They will listen to nighttime noises, and discover how it feels to sleep upon the ground. Not incidentally, these camping experiences will create a special kind of family intimacy.

Help Boys Learn About Bicycle Repair

While the yesteryear stereotype of men endlessly tinkering in the garage is limiting in many ways, I have discovered that countless boys who run into problems with their bikes don't know how to perform basic maintenance or repairs, such as oiling or replacing a bike chain, maintaining tire pressure and changing a flat tire. With time boys will learn to overhaul their hub, as well as how to take wheels apart and clean ball bearings. If there is no bicycle enthusiast in your home to teach these basic skills, you may discover that sometimes people at local bike shops can help, or they may even offer a course. It's also likely that boys who can fix their own bikes, or skateboards or skimboards, just might learn more sense of confidence and self-reliance.

Exposure to Nature Teaches Awareness of Life's Interconnectedness

Children who have developed an appreciation for nature at an early age will also come to understand how nature seeks balance; that leaves die in the fall but renewal comes in the spring; that honeybees may sting but without them there would be no pollination. Nature provides abundant examples of decay and destruction but also of regeneration and renewal. Exposure to the never-ending cycle of birth, life, death and rebirth in nature can put life and death into perspective and impart a sense of constancy in a changing world. Nature's strong regenerative ability also teaches that damage can be healed.

Plant a Garden

Children who are able to pick peas fresh from the garden likely do not have to be coaxed to eat their vegetables, and children who get involved in gardening may also develop an appreciation for healthy eating that stays with them. Most kids learn best through hands-on experiences, and digging in the damp soil—whether in your yard, a community garden, or even a small container garden on a patio or balcony—imparts sensory pleasure while also teaching about the cycles of nature, and about where food comes from. Together, you might also plant indigenous flowers to attract butterflies and hummingbirds into your yard, and later study the seeds and the plants at their different stages of maturity.

Welcome the Birds

Thoughtfully placed birdhouses will bring hours of enjoyment to your family as you observe feeding patterns throughout the day. Be sure to place a bird feeder near a window so that you can make observations from within the home. Make pinecone bird feeders with peanut butter and birdseed and hang in local trees. Children love to watch the birds that peck the small holes as well as the ground feeders who are too big for the feeder and so gather around the bottom to munch the fallen seeds. As you continue this practice throughout the year, and the weather gets colder, your family will be drawn even closer to nature as they observe the birds' elemental quest for survival.

Children Learn What They Live

When kids gain the ability to safely navigate their immediate outdoor surroundings, they develop confidence in the larger world and the belief that they will be eventually able to lead their own lives. Learning about the environment from an early age introduces boys to a range of experiences and perhaps even potential career opportunities they might not otherwise consider. Children who always walk on pavement might never think of becoming a wildlife conservationist, a horticulturist, or a marine biologist unless they are introduced to untamed wilderness, taken for a walk in the woods or to the seaside. Remember too that spending time together out-of-doors is a wonderful way to strengthen bonds within families. Outdoor activities can teach children trust, teamwork, and the satisfaction of achievement—that each family member is vital to the group's overall success.

Protecting the Environment

Today's children will inherit the most technologically advanced society ever witnessed on this planet. They will communicate with each other in ways we can't yet imagine, at speeds that will boggle our minds, exchanging information that hasn't yet been discovered. Schools can provide some education about the environment, but it is a personal connection to the environment that leads to an appreciation for the importance of the ways that as we are nourished and sustained by green spaces, we must in turn sustain these spaces in our lives.

Leonardo da Vinci once said: "Human subtlety will never devise an invention more beautiful, more simple or more direct than does nature, because in her inventions nothing is lacking and nothing is superfluous." May you and your children take more time this summer to get outside and experience the healing powers of nature. When your children becoming increasingly active outside, you might just find yourself doing more laundry, bandaging more knees, or even tripping over creepy crawlies brought inside for scientific examination—but your kids will be growing strong and healthy, and, with a bit of luck, happily tired for a night of restorative sleep.

QUESTIONS ABOUT BOYS & SCHOOLS
• • • • • • • •

I have had countless conversations with educators about ways that our approaches to schooling can be re-vitalized in order to maintain the interest and motivation of students. Many question the current effectiveness of archaic old-school solutions. Many express doubts about the effectiveness and wisdom of automatic sanctions and disciplinary measures such as suspension for typical misbehaviours such as swearing, defiance, fighting, smoking, and even truancy. Committed and caring professionals, tell me that focussing on boys' behaviour alone is futile, and bypasses real problems. Many of these educators also recognize that in today's rapid-fire electronic digital age, traditional classroom learning which emphasizes lock-step instruction practised through drill and repetition, invariably assessed through written means, often does not work.

Above all, I have learned that caring educators know they cannot help boys on their own. The teachers I talk to deeply want to collaborate with parents, and engage the wider community. They want to meet with parents and other community leaders to discuss how each adult experiences a particular boy in a particular way so they can work together to broaden their understanding about a particular boy's needs. They want to generate shared action that is positive and productive—leading to optimistic outcomes.

Do Boys Lack Motivation?

Recently, a mother consulted me about her 13 year old son's poor classroom behaviour and poor school achievement. She recited a laundry list of the teacher's complaints: Michael frequently blurts out answers without raising his hand first. He gets up and wanders around the classroom when he is supposed to be sitting at his desk. He struggles to pay attention. He will read comics but not novels. His handwriting is messy. His desk is disorganized. He makes rude and sarcastic comments to his classmates about assignments he doesn't like. His written answers are short and skimpy. He does the least to get by. He seems more interested in recess and his informal hockey league than his formal education. She pleaded with me, "What am I to do?"

Wondering if Michael has a problem with learning, Wendy blamed herself. She expressed misgiving about her parenting. Maybe she didn't read to him enough when he was young. Perhaps she should have expected more from him, that he practise his spelling more rather than go outside to play. Probably she should have insisted that her husband be more engaged with his homework. She also worried that her son would turn away from schooling like her husband did at a similar age.

As we settled into discussing her son's academic needs and behaviour challenges, Wendy revealed to me the teacher comment she struggled with the most: "Your son lacks self-motivation."

Wendy's disappointment and self-blame turned to blame of the school. "My son has been motivated since birth," she explained. "He spends countless hours building or perfecting his latest bike manoeuvre, and weeks getting to the next level on his favourite video game." She elaborated how Michael recently worked alongside his father to build a new wooden deck in the backyard despite miserable weather conditions. While his carpentry skills did not match his father's, he behaved as though his contribution did. Michael worked quietly, diligently, giving his best effort—even offering suggestions to unforeseen problems. Like a momma bear protecting her cub, Wendy then looked directly into my eyes and asserted, "My son does not lack self-motivation. That is not the problem. School is the problem. The school's unrealistic expectations are the problem. I want your help to get my son back on track."

As a longtime educator and counsellor, I have learned first-hand that Wendy's complaint is more common than many of our learning communities would like to admit.

Many parents have questions about boys and schooling. The challenge for both parents and teachers is not to become reactive, defensive, or take sides, but to appreciate that motivation operates differently in each child. While some boys become eager to participate at the mere mention of outdoor physical activity, others withdraw, preferring to work alone inside. It may be more likely that boys will become more motivated than girls to play video games, but not always. At times it may be tempting to make sweeping claims about boys' behaviour, but if we want to influence motivation, we must understand that each child is unique. This section highlights questions related to boys and schooling that matter most to parents.

16   Concerns About ADHD

MANY parents wonder when the expression of a boy's high spirits and energy is natural and healthy, and when it seems excessive and even abnormal. The following email from a parent expresses familiar concerns about the implications of an ADHD label.

Is ADHD the automatic default label when boys struggle with attention in schools?

Dear Barry,

My 9 year old boy struggles to sit for long periods of time and moves around the classroom more than last year's teacher liked. He'd also rush through his written work, be messy and make careless mistakes. While these behaviours are somewhat typical for him, in previous years I'd discuss with his teachers creative ways to sustain his attention and work with his hectic energy.

To my surprise, last year's teacher didn't want to brainstorm ideas with me but instead suggested that I have my doctor assess my son for attention problems. She added that after the school had the doctor's results, we would meet to discuss what could be done in the classroom. Uncertain about the details of what led her to seek medical advice, I pressed her for more information. I was hoping we'd join forces, but she assured me that her procedure was intended to rule out medical conditions first. She indicated that after the doctor looked at both our

Conners' Rating Scales, he would establish a diagnosis and then we'd discuss educational interventions at the school.

Is this a new approach that I don't know about—rule out ADHD first?

Fearing that the school staff might label my boy as hyperactive, I took my son to see our family doctor who was quite frankly annoyed with the teacher's request and indicated that he didn't see any attention problems. He sent me back to the school to find solutions. He indicated that a small percentage of parents and teachers would rather assess for ADHD or even medicate a child first rather than take the tiresome steps to explore altering home or learning environments. He made it very clear that he does prescribe ADHD medication for children, but only after a variety of heartfelt and thoughtful approaches have first been tried.

Relieved that my son did not have ADHD, I returned to the school but was stunned when the teacher suggested I persist with our family doctor and seek a referral to a pediatrician for a more complete assessment before we could discuss anything further at school.

I know that class sizes have grown and teachers deal with many more children with special needs than ever before, but I worry that kids who just can't hold it down might be seen as more disruptive. It just seems to me that seeking advice from experts outside the classroom before exploring options inside the classroom is hasty. Am I off track here? I don't want to get a reputation as an uncooperative parent who blames others for their child's problems.

Jessica

Dear Jessica,

The **National Institute of Mental Health** estimates that about three to five percent of children have legitimate ADHD, yet the numbers of prescriptions vary widely from place to place. The **World Health Organization** declared the use of stimulant drugs to manage behaviour to be at epidemic levels internationally in 2001. Many are concerned that spontaneity, inquisitiveness, imagination, boundless enthusiasm, and emotionality are being discouraged to create calmer, quieter, more controlled environments.

Parents especially become alarmed when they learn that drugs such as *Ritalin* and *Concerta* prescribed for ADHD are central nervous system stimulants and share many of the pharmacological effects of amphetamine, methamphetamine, and cocaine. They may also worry about the potential for *Ritalin* abuse, which is widespread among adolescents who sell their *Ritalin* on the street. Even worse, parents wonder whether drug intervention will actually help their son perform better academically—or does it merely make him easier to manage during the hours that the mediation is working? In the long run, are students any better off? Concerns have also been expressed about the process of diagnosing ADHD, and about how treatment by prescription can deemphasize parental roles, as well as everyday common-sense interventions.

Whatever we think about the basis of ADHD—neurobiological, artificially manufactured syndrome, or somewhere in between—it is something that we who are concerned about the school success of boys cannot ignore. We can also not ignore the significance of the fact that among children labelled hyperactive, boys outnumber girls by at least four to one.

The topic of ADHD presents an additional quagmire that has a bearing on your situation because each of the symptoms that are supposed to lead to a diagnosis of ADHD—restlessness, impulsiveness, and difficulty paying attention—occurs commonly in children who have entirely different problems, and is also typical for many children in general—especially boys.

To speak directly to your question about whether ruling out ADHD first is a new school approach, I can be very succinct: No.

Work Toward Solutions, Not Accentuating Problems

In my experience it is unusual for a teacher to suggest a medical or psychiatric diagnosis before first seeking collaborative solutions. Parents and teachers who collaborate at the outset may work toward finding solutions rather than accentuating problems.

Some adults who have not been in classrooms for decades may assume that if children are sitting quietly, good teaching must be happening. Experienced and skilled teachers, however, recognize that a quiet classroom does not necessarily signal deep learning. The skillful teachers I have talked to have learned to channel rambunctious behaviour in creative and productive ways. They do not penalize poor handwriting, and look beyond messy and disorganized schoolwork as they find ways to encourage boys academically. Experienced teachers also know that a medical diagnosis or drugs should not be the first option in the treatment of behaviour characterized as ADHD. They know that children who struggle with their attention respond favourably to a consistent, structured environment with clear rules, engaging and active classroom inquiry, and flexible classroom or individual adaptations that often end up helping other students too. These teachers may, for example, break learning tasks down into smaller, more discrete steps; they make sure that they have the child's attention when they give directions that are both spoken and written; they may find one-on-one tutors, note-takers, or peer helpers for the student; they may give the disruptive student a responsibility; they often arrange subtle reminder cues or hand signals with these students; they teach organizational skills.

Teachers also recognize that developmental differences exist among children, and that for some boys in particular, sitting down, listening, and completing written assignments are going to be more difficult in a traditional classroom setting. Furthermore, they appreciate how behaviours characterized as disruptive often disappear when a child is watching TV, playing a video game, or engaged in free play. They are aware that the way a child's environment is organized and the way tasks are presented can mean the difference between what is perceived as within the range of normal and what is labelled as attention deficit.

Just as parents—or any of us for that matter—can misread situations, it is possible that the teacher who blocked collaboration with you may have a misunderstanding about diagnosing ADHD. On the odd occasion I meet teachers and parents who do not recognize that a score on the *Conners' Rating Scales*—parent and teacher questionnaires about how they each see a child's behaviour—, or any of the other scales used in diagnosis, gives the appearance of scientific precision, as though it were, say, a blood test. In reality, the score is nothing more than a numerical value that sums up a particular parent or teacher's subjective judgments about the child's level of impulsivity, inattention, and hyperactivity. They are intended as guidelines to explore whether a child might display ADHD criteria and to be useful AFTER reasonable discussions and a variety of approaches have first been considered.

It is unfortunate that the psychiatrists who design the research, shape the diagnostic categories, develop questionnaires and rating scales, and prescribe the drugs, rarely question what kind of attitudes adults hold toward boisterous kids. I suspect that some teachers and parents who find fewer hyperactive children in their classrooms and homes may work hard to design appropriate tasks for children who might otherwise squirm, and may be more tolerant of what is loosely considered *off-task behaviour* by others.

There is also the curious concern with parents who rate their child differently on the *Conners' Rating Scales* from the teacher at school. As it turns out, simple subjectivity is not the answer. The reality is that children act differently in different places. There is no test or assessment instrument that can unequivocally determine ADHD or the medical view of a biochemical imbalance, let alone the magic line that differentiates the groups.

Considerable Attention Required Before Diagnosis

It might also be helpful for you to know that even researchers who are comfortable with both the diagnosis of ADHD and prescribing of stimulant medication for children have urged that considerable care to be taken in the process of diagnosis and deciding who stimulant medication is best suited for.

There are many theories about what causes attention deficit, and why diagnoses are so much on the increase now. Some look to genetic influences, nutrition, environmental pollutants, and so forth. Medical researchers reporting in *Lancet,* for example, have concluded that common food additives and colourings can increase hyperactive behaviour in a large number of children. In today's world some of our foods are not really even foods, but synthetics products made from artificial ingredients, causing our bodies to work harder to eliminate pollutants in our environment. I am not suggesting that this is a root cause with your son, but only offer it as an example to emphasize just how complicated it can be to understand why children struggle with attention.

Of course, ADHD is a mental health diagnosis that won't simply vanish. Given the pressures on the school systems to improve mandated services for students struggling with behavioural and learning difficulties, it is not surprising that ADHD is being overly diagnosed in places. While there are some cases in which children need, and benefit from, a comprehensive diagnosis and treatment plan for ADHD, there is a tendency to give the diagnosis too quickly, without thorough psycho-educational assessment, and without exploration of alternative approaches or modifications first.

So what is a parent to do?

Focus on Positive Plans of Action

Recognize that while educators can be strong advocates for students grappling with maintaining focus, behaviour, or achievement, teachers cannot do it alone. A parent is a child's best advocate.

It seems that you have been an effective supporter over the years, but have been stumped with this recent experience. Informal parent-teacher meetings provide the best forum to learn about your child's education so that you may partner with his teachers to identify small improvements as you both mentor your son for success.

I would like to underline *informal discussions* here. Many parents email me that they feel overwhelmed at formal school discussions such as school-based team meetings where several school staff are present, including the school psychologist. But remember that teachers do not have medical training, and that school psychologists are not regular psychologists, nor psychiatrists. Typically, school psychologists are teachers who have a master's degree in educational testing and are highly skilled in measuring student abilities with standardized tests.

While they are an important part of the educational team, it is important for parents to not over-estimate the authority of testing data from psychometric tests.

Sometimes parents who feel frustrated and overwhelmed bring angry accusations into these discussions, making matters worse. I can tell by your comments that you have skills as a communicator and have no doubt avoided exacerbating potential conflict. It's seems that you have struck a balance between being sympathetic to your son, yet respectful of the teacher at the same time.

While I would certainly wait and see how your son responds in Grade 4 this fall, if the Grade 4 teacher raises similar concerns about disruptive classroom behaviours, be sure to ask for specifics.

Seek objective details about what the teacher has done to accommodate your son's learning style. Objective language describes in precise, neutral terms what your son does, when he does it, and how frequently he does it. If the teacher uses words like *off-task*, *hyperactive,* or *zoned out*, avoid becoming overwhelmed by these subjective, judgmental labels that only invite defensive reactions. Do note that teachers should be able to tell you about several things that have been tried to help your child be successful. Be sure to contribute by pointing out what you have found to be successful in the past. Mostly, keep your discussion focussed on your child's learning, recognizing that it is a teacher's job to respond to varying learning styles and needs.

If the teacher is uncooperative seek help. School officials know that teachers are only human and can at times make mistakes and have developed communication protocols for minimizing conflicts while keeping student needs front and center. Authorities recognize that we need a holistic approach that does not pit educators and parents against each other, but maintains a clear focus on finding positive plans of action.

Parents and teachers may look at children's learning from different perspectives, but they share a common goal—making sure that children receive the best education possible. Respectful communication between home and school takes advantage of both perspectives to provide children with the kind of care and education that will help them thrive. In an atmosphere of mutual respect, we can discuss highly charged issues around boys and learning and work collaboratively for success.

17   Auditory Processing Challenges

WHILE there can be many reasons why boys may have difficulty concentrating, an often-overlooked possibility is a struggle with incoming auditory demands. As sound waves travel through the ear and are changed into electrical information, the incoming sound information can become interrupted for some people as the brain struggles to process what has been said. Understandably, children can lose confidence and become insecure when they are not aware of the source of the problem. Boys especially become restless, withdrawn and isolated. Rather than sinking into feelings of incompetence, many boys become disruptive. They can even appear to have difficulties paying attention and be misdiagnosed with ADHD.

What happens when a boy can hear sounds well enough but struggles with making sense of their meaning?

Dear Barry,

When all is calm and quiet, my son seems to be able to listen and focus, but add outside noise or background sounds in the room and he seems to lose focus. His kindergarten teacher indicates that he doesn't follow directions easily and that he frequently needs them repeated. I recently got his hearing checked at the **Health Unit** and they said that he hears well, yet I can't help but think that something is still wrong. A friend told me about your workshop and she said that sometimes there is a reason why kids hear but can't make sense of what they hear. Any suggestions would be helpful.

Ramona

Dear Ramona,

What children hear and interpret has a huge impact on how they learn and behave. Language moulds our sense of who we are and helps us understand how we think, work, and play and influences the nature of our relationships.

As you consider your son's situation, maybe a story about another boy who I worked with and also had difficulty with listening at times will be helpful.

A boy named Josh has a tough time with learning and social interaction in kindergarten. Give him one task and he can carry it through. Give Josh three and his eyes glaze over. His teacher complains that he is frequently inattentive, restless and prone to angry outbursts. His parents, worried that his rocky start may sour him on school, request a meeting with his teacher and the school counsellor to explore possibilities to help their son.

Despite their embarrassment about Josh's learning difficulties, they find that the meeting really gets them thinking. Initially they fear that the staff will request a medical assessment for ADHD, but instead they discover tremendous concern for their son and his learning difficulties.

Their shared discussion increases their understanding of his strengths and challenges at home and school. A wide-ranging exchange leads to insight about his difficulties and his ups and downs at school. Together they realize that Josh is suffering from serious information overload.

The school counsellor indicates that while for many boys the combination of fewer connecting fibers between hemispheres and a more compartmentalized brain results in the need to attend to one instruction at a time, Josh struggles more than most boys in this regard. She suggests that he may have an auditory processing problem.

She elaborates that for most of us making sense of what we hear seems straightforward, but that listening might be hindered for Josh. She goes on to suggest that it is little wonder he becomes unruly and stubborn as he struggles to listen and cope with the overwhelm of incoming auditory demands. She also indicates that males can have difficulty discriminating what they hear when background noise—as in a noisy restaurant—is present. She adds that auditory processing difficulties are also recognized as a major factor with dyslexia.

Auditory processing difficulties are more common among boys. Despite most having excellent hearing many just do not process the entirety of what they hear. They may process part, but without processing the rest, often the whole meaning is lost, or they perceive a totally incorrect idea of what has been said. They may even be able to repeat back word for word without understanding the intended meaning. If conversation has a high emotional content, understanding can be even more difficult.

Questions for Considering Possible Auditory Processing Problem

The school counsellor asks several questions that really help get to the heart of Josh's difficulty with learning:

- Are conversations hard for Josh to follow—especially in certain situations?
- Is Josh easily distracted or unusually bothered by loud or sudden noises?
- Does Josh have difficulty following directions—whether straightforward or complicated?
- Does Josh often ask for repetition or clarification?
- Is he disorganized & forgetful?
- Does his behaviour and performance improve in quieter settings?

Note: This checklist of questions does not form a diagnosis.

The blur of background noise or multi-step directions can interfere with some children's ability to process language. These processing difficulties are typically marked by difficulties with decoding phonics, comprehending what is read, and especially with following directions.

While school staffs are often first to suspect auditory processing difficulties, a diagnosis warrants a battery of audiometric tests, administered by an audiologist who is qualified to determine if hearing is impaired, and to what degree. Check with your son's school for a screening process.

Types of Auditory Processing Problems

1. **Auditory discrimination**—the ability to notice, isolate, compare, distinguish distinct and separate sounds in words. When sounds cannot be isolated, people may hear "turn left at the wall" instead of "turn left down the hall."

2. **Auditory figure-ground discrimination**—the ability to pick out important sounds from a noisy background. Children may claim that background noise is too loud as they generally struggle to separate words spoken by their teacher from sounds of children talking in the classroom or traffic outside.

3. **Auditory memory**—the ability to store and recall both short term and long term information when given verbally. Children may find it difficult to remember telephone numbers, names and follow multi-step directions.

4. **Auditory sequencing**—the ability to remember or reconstruct order of items in lists or order of sounds in a word or syllable. A child may hear *ephelant* for *elephant* and struggle with persistent spelling problems.

5. **Auditory blending**—the process of putting together phonemes or sounds to form words. Problems with auditory blending can make it difficult to accurately spell words phonetically.

What Can Teachers Do at School?

1. **Reduce background noise**—including air conditioning and heating systems, traffic, playground, hallway, computers, and fans. Reduce acoustical echoing within the classroom—consider adding room dividers, bookshelves, acoustic tiles, carpet, wall hangings, and sound absorbing bulletin boards.

2. **Consider a seating plan** that will maximize benefits from auditory and visual cues. Assigned seats should be away from the hall and street noise and not more than two metres from the teacher. Provide an optional quiet study area such as a study carrel. Assign a listening buddy.

3. **Gain the child's attention** before giving directions. Emphasize key words when speaking or writing especially when presenting new information. Pre-instruction with emphasis on the main ideas to be presented may also be useful.

4. **Provide brief verbal directions.** Allow opportunities for students to collaborate with each other to clarify instructions. Before speaker begins, find a

novel way to attract students' attention and pause to allow time to catch up and process information. Identify key vocabulary on the board when covering new material and ensure that discussion centers on these words.

5. **Increase visual prompts.** Provide instructions through physical demonstrations as visual messages may be much easier to store in memory. Strengthen communication with non-verbal and visual cues such as pictures, diagrams, illustrations, mindmaps and flowcharts. Use body gestures that will clarify information.

6. **Provide frequent breaks** and opportunities to relax. Learning is hindered by fatigue, often leading to frustration. Remember that children with auditory processing challenges will expend more effort in paying attention and discriminating information than most students.

7. **Avoid showing frustration** when the child misunderstands a message.

8. **Avoid asking the child to listen and write at the same time.**

9. **Physical activity** assists the brain to process and integrate learning.

10. **With professional support,** consider whether an auditory trainer may be useful. Auditory trainers are electronic devices that allow a person to focus attention on a speaker and reduce the interference of background noise. Teachers can wear a microphone to transmit sound and the student wears a headset to receive his teacher's instructions more clearly.

It is important to note that when listening hinders learning, these problems rarely occur in isolation. A boy who is not able to keep in check unwanted background sounds might also struggle with focussing his eyes or tracking smoothly across the page for easy reading. A sound distortion can also be compounded by temporary hearing losses from middle ear infections or allergic congestion.

The root causes of auditory difficulties are not well understood and can include chronic ear infections, head trauma, lead poisoning and a myriad of unknown reasons. Because there are many different possibilities—even combinations of causes—it is best for children to be assessed on an individual basis.

18   Parent-Teacher Conferences

PARENT-TEACHER conferences are an important component of ongoing home–school communication, but sometimes they are easier than others.In parent-teacher conferences, teachers and parents reach out to communicate about how they can work together to best support their child. But what happens if the chemistry at a parent-teacher conference seems off? The following email from a parent identifies a common pitfall with communication that can leave both parents and teachers working at cross-purposes.

How can parent-teacher conferences be more productive?

Dear Barry,

Report card time is just around the corner and soon I will be meeting with my boy's Grade 4 teacher at a conference. She sent home a special note requesting to meet with me about my son, Justin. While this may sound silly, I feel as though my son is a burden and I am really uneasy about talking with her. Last year my husband and I met with his Grade 3 teacher but did not find the meeting helpful. While last year's teacher talked on about how Justin was underachieving and acting up, I never really got a clear picture about what was going on in the classroom. It's like there was this divide with our communication. My husband called it jargon. I called it exasperating. We almost walked out of the meeting when she said that our son took more than 1/26th of her time. The more questions we asked to better understand what was going on, the more I felt misunderstood. I don't want to assume that the upcoming parent-teacher conference will be the same, but I worry that it will get off track again. I'd appreciate some tools to maintain clear communication.

Lynne

Dear Lynne,

While it is normal for parents to be a bit nervous when their children are struggling in school, they can relax more when they remember that teachers are professionals who benefit from the input of parents.

Teachers know that their job is to meet the needs of all children, and to pay particular attention to youth who struggle with learning or behaviour. Let go any anxiety you may have about your son being a burden in the classroom. Remember that it is a teacher's job to respond to varying learning styles and needs.

Children have their own individual personalities, and their own listening and work habits. To help students learn new knowledge and skills, teachers must know as much as they can about each child's learning preferences. No one knows more about these things than a parent. Teachers and parents can work together to support your son in his learning and social interactions.

Over the years I have noticed that meetings can be derailed by frustration and defensiveness caused by unclear communication.

Use Neutral Factual Language to Describe Concerns

During the meeting be aware of the words you use to describe your son. Try to use neutral, factual language to describe behaviour and achievement rather than interpretive, subjective language. When parents and teachers use charged or subjective terms, the other party may get confused, defensive, even reactive.

In the following examples, notice how subjective and evaluative words are likely to create distance, defensiveness, and confusion. In contrast, neutral and factual words focus on what actually happened so that people get a clear picture:

Subjective 1—"Tommy is so immature and disruptive."

Objective 1—"Tommy gets out of his seat and walks around the classroom every ten or fifteen minutes."

Subjective 2—"Tyler is rude and uncooperative. I don't know what to do with him."

Objective 2—"When asked to complete the assignment in class, Tyler told me in front of all the students, "You can't make me do this," and "This class is totally boring.""

Subjective 3—"Adam daydreams and seems scattered—he must be ADHD!"

Objective 3—"While I am talking, Adam stares out the window for periods of about five minutes until I quietly ask him how it's going."

Objective language describes in precise, neutral terms what the boy does, when he does it, and how frequently he does it. Subjective, judgmental labels only invite defensive reactions.

Rather than giving the impression that a boy is incorrigible—or worse, unteachable—teachers anticipate success by using clear, non-labelling language that facilitates productive discussion with a focus on constructive action.

A Two-Way Conversation

Like all good conversations, parent-teacher conferences are best when both people talk and listen. The conference is a time for you to learn about your child's progress in school. It is also a time for the teacher to learn about what your child is like at home. When you tell the teacher about your son's skills, interests, needs, and dreams, the teacher can help your son more.

Maintain Emphasis on Learning

Productive parent–teacher conferences focus on how well the child is doing in school. They also talk about how the child can do even better. To get ready for the conversation, look at your son's recent assignments, projects, and tests, before the conference. You might bring a list of questions that you would like to ask the teacher.

Be ready to ask questions about ways you and the teacher can help your son with some of his challenges:

- What kind of projects and assignments do you anticipate my son will be enthusiastic about or find difficult?

- How will these assignments be evaluated?

- What can I do at home to enhance what is happening in the classroom?

- What if my son struggles and falls behind? What if he learns quickly and then gets bored? How do you accommodate differences in learning?

A Process for More In-depth Dialogue

Despite a parent and teacher's best intentions, recognize that at times a child's needs may warrant a more in-depth discussion. It is for this reason that educator and parent advocacy groups have developed a process like the following checklist I often use to ensure that students receive optimal support:

1. Teacher and parent meet to clarify concern. If a problem has been brewing for some time, you can suspect that your child's teacher has carefully read your son's student file and will likely have consulted with previous teachers and support staff before your meeting. Of course, it is not uncommon for a teacher to obtain more in-depth information after a preliminary meeting with you.

Expect to discuss how each of you experiences your son in different environments and circumstances; for example, the teacher will be able to discuss informal recess and unstructured activity observations providing parents with valuable information about a child's social world. Parents in turn can provide details about early development and social experiences that teachers will likely not be aware of.

Be certain to discuss a child's health in general. Does he struggle with allergies, sleep, anxiety or shyness? Taking a step back from a presenting concern will help to gain perspective and understanding of the whole child, not just the problem. If health concerns are present, seek a medical assessment if one has not been completed in recent times.

2. Discuss strategies and interventions currently being used at home and in the classroom. Parents and teachers should both know what each has done to support a child to overcome a particular difficulty. You need to learn about what adaptations have been made to the curriculum and or the environment. You can also offer your experience with any strategies you have tried at home, and help the teacher better understand your son's needs.

You should also learn about any additional staff who, under the teacher's direction, have become involved with your son. A classroom teacher will also share with you the perspectives that other staff—such as a learning support teacher—have to offer.

I have also learned that it can be helpful for parents to meet the support staff member who works with their son. While we can all appreciate that each staff member has a different background and experience, we know that what matters most is the fit between the particular child and the particular staff member.

3. Whenever possible, engage and involve your son in discussions about his progress. Sometimes a calm discussion not focussed on disciplinary measures can lead to insight that can takes months to acquire without a child's input.

4. Discuss whether additional input from a school counsellor may help. As trained classroom teachers with an advanced degree in counselling psychology, school counsellors are valuable resources to help parents and teachers make sense of issues that children commonly struggle with. Rather than expecting the school counsellor to automatically become a therapist for your son, invite his or her input to become a part of your son's support and strengthening team. Sometimes this involves meeting and briefly working with a child and then reporting back to the parent and teacher, and sometimes a school counsellor can immediately contribute to better understanding a particular child's learning and behaviour without direct counselling intervention. The school counsellor can stimulate further discussion, helping to generate ideas and suggestions not yet considered.

5. Make a plan to ensure accountability. It is important for both parent and teacher to hold each other accountable by maintaining and discussing each of your ongoing perceptions about your son's response to your interventions.

6. Consider input from other school staff members. If several weeks have passed and concerns persist, discuss a referral to the *School-based Team*—commonly abbreviated to **SBT**. A SBT serves to expand thinking about how to support your child best by drawing on the input of staff with differing expertise. Be aware that in most cases parents need to grant permission for staff to meet and discuss a child's progress as a SBT. As gatekeepers, with government rules to follow, SBT discussions can, in the worst cases, become simply a team deciding where to allocate resources, and whether or not to place your child on a list to receive a battery of educational-psychology tests to help determine if he has an undiagnosed learning disability. More typically, though, I have experienced SBT's as a rich untapped resource of knowledge about how to help children thrive.

It is possible that the SBT may wish to access district resources, such as a behaviour consultant, or refer you to community professional, such as a pediatrician. These professionals can all support your son in different ways, but none should detract from the positive plan of action generated by the parent, the teacher, and the SBT.

Be alert for the possibility that input from those who do not fully understand the complexity of your son's circumstances may unwittingly contribute to his discouragement. Thus it is crucial for you as a parent to speak up if someone makes a recommendation that doesn't make sense to you.

7. Provide active support for your son. After the SBT has made some preliminary recommendations, consider whether you understand and feel comfortable with them. At times you might find that you only need more time to consider the recommendation, and other times you will recognize when the recommendation is just off the mark. As you advocate for your son, trust your inner wisdom while you also remain receptive to learning new information and approaches.

8. Monitor progress. Like your own family home, classrooms are busy places with new and varied needs cropping up daily. Follow-up meetings must be set up, where you and other caring support people can explore what is helping and what is hindering your son's progress. After giving a particular approach enough time to be tried and tested, be prepared to make adjustments or revisions if warranted.

19   Recess Matters

SCHOOLS have not been immune to the fear of litigation that has seeped into our society—on the contrary, they have been a focal point, and no teacher or administrator relishes the thought of being sued. It's true that accidents can happen while kids cavort in recess and lunchtime play. But some school districts have become so self-protective that they have banned tag, touch football, and other rough-and-tumble activities. In recent years many parents have expressed their wish that playground accidents be treated as accidents—not as excuses to exploit well-intentioned schools to the full extent of the law. Many parents and teachers wonder how children can grow up capable of making decisions for themselves about work, life and play, when their caregivers seek to regulate their every move. They want to know whether we can simply learn to accept a few bumps and bruises as a natural part of vigourous childhood play.

The following email expresses a parental frustration: "Don't the kids who struggle with behaviour and learning NEED recess the most?"

How can freestyle recess and lunchtime games energize children for learning and help them develop social and self-management skills?

Why Recess Is Not Mere Child's Play

> **Dear Barry,**
>
> My Grade 4 son Travis misses recess and lunch play breaks on a regular basis for acting up in class and not completing his work. His teacher claims he needs to make up the time and that he will benefit from the extra practice.

I strongly believe that making Travis miss his playtime will not make him smarter or more attentive in class. He's the kind of boy that gets cranky, unfocussed, and irritable when he doesn't get a chance to be active, and run around and play. He needs to get up and move!

To me, it makes so much sense that after kids spend extended time sitting in the classroom they need playtime to cut loose, and do their own thing, like the rest of us. After all, we require our workplaces to give a break to adults, so why would we not require the same for our kids? Shouldn't there be a school regulation protecting recess and lunch breaks for kids?

Surely, our schools have evolved beyond my own childhood memories of traditional classroom learning where if a student didn't finish math problems by the time the buzzer went off, they missed recess; or if someone coughed or sneezed when the teacher wanted silence, the whole class missed recess.

I would appreciate what your experience and research says about the value of recess for children and learning. Don't the kids who struggle with behaviour and learning need recess the most?

Michelle

Dear Michelle,

Over the past decade an alarming numbers of schools have been cutting back on recess playtime or eliminating it altogether. At the same time, school suspensions, behaviour problems in school, and childhood obesity are on the rise. Like you, many wonder why children who struggle with attention or misbehaviour at school are punished by having to miss recess. What's going on here?

You don't have to look too far to read alarming headlines about the math, science, and reading scores of American students falling behind the scores of students in other countries. Mandates to correct this perceived gap in achievement have pressured school districts to show improved academic achievement through standardized testing. As efforts turn to raising achievement scores, recess, along with the creative arts—music, drama, dance and play—may be seen as disposable luxuries. After all, how do you measure the success of listening to music, experimenting with colour and light while painting, or playing an unstructured game during a recess or lunch break?

Yet, recognizing the positive role that unstructured play has in the healthy development of children, many educational authorities around the globe have taken a different approach. Did you know that Swiss elementary-aged students are given a brief five minute unstructured recess break every hour, or that in New Zealand and Australia, there must be a minimum of ninety minutes per week of unstructured recess? Many experts today are emphasizing that children need free play. The benefits include reduction in stress-related illness, obesity, irritability, loss of sleep, attention problems, and school burnout.

Recess Bullied by Pressures to Succeed

In our high-pressured culture, parents often fear that if their children are not well prepared and high achieving, they will not get a desired spot in higher education. Some very young kids who are enrolled in piano lessons, test-prep enrichment courses, digital media courses, and sports activities seem to be building their college resumes by the time they start kindergarten. Despite evidence indicating that excessive pressure to achieve is likely to manifest in somatic symptoms and school avoidance, the selection for private pre-school programs in some communities can be fiercely competitive; anxious parents are encouraged to carefully groom their sons for the intake interview.

Not surprisingly, these pressures lead many parents and teachers to believe that increasing the time children spend in explicit learning will increase their chances of school success. Some adults may imagine that kids' grades can be boosted in any spare scrap of time that can be found during the day: kids can bow to books after school in learning centres, in the evening for homework, or even during recess periods and lunchtime. What if the evidence suggested otherwise? What if we discovered that while learning takes time, providing more time to learn does not ensure that more learning will take place?

A **Stanford** study ranked those school reforms that seemed to increase school achievement the most: peer tutoring, smaller classes, increased use of computers, and adding an hour of instruction to each day. The study found that more time spent learning ranked fourth.

According to Frank Smith, the author of *Insult to Intelligence*: "When learning is meaningful we learn much faster...Having to spend long periods of time in repetitive efforts to learn specific things is a sign that learning is not taking place, that we are not in a productive learning situation." While practice may lead to great improvement when children are passionate about developing a particular talent—like playing an electric guitar or ice hockey—additional time spent in traditional learning is more likely to turn students off. Rather than watching slow hands of the clock, students who get a chance to go outside and run around can release stress and get re-energized.

Most elementary teachers I have met testify to the benefits of giving breaks to children who have been sitting for a long time. Most teachers know all too well that without breaks students—especially boys—become restless, fidgety, and trouble-prone. As Dr. Olga Jarrett, a child development specialist, reports: "Fourth-Graders were more on-task, less fidgety and less disruptive in the classroom on days when they had recess, with hyperactive children among those who benefited the most." In order to reduce attention and behavioural problems, Dr. Jarrett concludes that recess breaks are essential.

Play Breaks Are Vital for Child Development

The *United Nations Convention on the Rights of the Child* even enshrines play as a specific human right for children, in addition to, and distinct from, a child's right to recreation and leisure. Both the **American Academy of Pediatrics** and the **Canadian Pediatric Society** claim that unstructured play is essential for maintaining optimal health, and for helping children reach important social, emotional, and cognitive developmental milestones. The **American Academy of Pediatrics** actively promotes free play "as a healthy, essential part of childhood...that all children are afforded ample, unscheduled, independent, non-screen time to be creative, to reflect, and to decompress...[and that] a large proportion of play should be child driven rather than adult directed." The **National Association of Early Childhood Specialists** even devotes an entire position paper to this issue entitled *Recess and the Importance of Play.* In their report, the **NAEC** states that unstructured recess play is a highly effective way to reduce students' stress and anxiety while increasing attention and focus.

Countless experts caution that reducing playtime at school recess and lunchtime will interfere with many facets of children's development. Free play allows children to develop competencies as they test and experiment with their fears in ways that are relatively non-threatening. Free play also supports other kinds of learning for children:

• the ability of children to problem-solve, make decisions, negotiate, and resolve conflict

• the exercise of creativity, ingenuity, and self-expression through the exchange of ideas

• the integration of social, emotional, physical, and academic learning through -out the school day

It might also be remarked that a teacher who watches a child in unstructured play develops greater capacity to understand that child.

Years of observing students at play have taught me first-hand that recess is not mere child's play. During recess breaks, children are in a peer setting where they can watch how others relate, experiment with being assertive, take appropriate risks, self-advocate, and test boundaries. With this knowledge, they are armed with greater self-confidence to go forth into the larger world.

Recent research also shows that providing a regular recess may actually help solve behavioural problems in class. Researchers from the **Albert Einstein College of Medicine** studied approximately 11,000 Third-Grade boys and girls enrolled in the national *Early Childhood Longitudinal Study* to discover what factors led to better school performance. Among the many factors studied, they considered children from two recess categories: those with fewer than fifteen minutes a day of recess and those with more than fifteen minutes a day. When classroom teachers were asked to rate their behaviours afterwards, they discovered that children who were cooped up during the day scored lower on behaviour scores. The lead researcher, Dr. Barros, concluded that it is a "big mistake" for teachers to punish a child for poor behaviour by denying recess. She emphasized that while adults may be able to concentrate for 45 to 60 minutes at a time, children need breaks more frequently. She also indicated that during recess, students "use all the things they learned in the classroom. When they are doing hopscotch they use math skills. Kids learn a lot about social skills during recess, such as playing, sharing, being the leader, following somebody. It's all very important."

Recess Play Teaches Self-Regulation

It also turns out that imaginative recess play allows children to make their own rules and practise self-control, a critical cognitive skill called executive function. While there are a number of different elements associated with executive function, the central one is the ability to self-regulate or control emotions and behaviour. This self-regulation, which includes resisting impulses and temptations, is of immediate and long-term benefit to children.

When children engage in imaginative recess play, they are also engaging in self-regulating private speech about what they are going to do and how they are going to do it. Researchers have discovered that children often use internal self-guiding comments recently picked up from their interactions with adults—"Easy does it. It's going to work out. Just wait a little bit longer."—signaling that they are beginning to apply the strategy of internal guiding self-talk.

Unlike structured play, free play gives children much more opportunity to practise this private self-talk, self-regulation, and internal control. In this way, recess provides opportunities for discovery learning. When there is no adult managing and directing, children learn more about delayed gratification, and waiting for gratification. Simple activities and children's self-organized games like **Man Hunt, Scary Monster**, or **Capture the Flag** also strengthen their relationships with each other.

According to Yale researcher Dr. Singer, school staffs are likely to underestimate the benefits of free play while accentuating fundamentals such as rote memorization and practice drills. Dr. Singer also points out that studies show children who are the most effective at complex imaginative play are also the ones most likely to cooperate with others without adult prompting and to take on social responsibilities. Free recess playtime trains children to deal with the unexpected and unscripted. It increases mental suppleness, and can help build a broader emotional and behavioural vocabulary.

Recess or Ritalin?

As brain science weighs in on the recess debate, evidence indicates that providing a change of pace in between learning activities enables the brain to focus better. This is why those of us adults with desk jobs requiring intense concentration may instinctively get up and clear our minds by doing something else for a bit. A recess break allows children who struggle with attention to expend their excess energy, making it easier to focus afterwards.

A study from **Washington State University** manipulated the brains of young rats to make them mimic the brains of children with ADHD, and found that rats with laboratory-induced attention problems played more frequently than rats whose brains had not been altered. The brain-altered rats were divided into two groups, those who were allowed to play as much as they wanted and those who were allowed only limited play, researchers discovered that the rats who were allowed ample opportunities for play did not become more wild, rambunctious or violent. Instead, they simply played normally and grew up to be non-hyperactive and socially well adjusted. The hyperactive rats who had limited opportunities for play developed socially troubling behaviours and had difficulty reading social cues from their rat peers. Research like this leads many to hypothesize that the restlessness seen in children with hyperactivity may simply be the child's way of expressing an innate need for more play.

Recognizing High-Spirited Youth During Recess and Lunch Breaks

Remarkable ideas are being considered and developed in our schools to more effectively meet the needs of students whose high-spirited, restlessness, or struggle with attention results in underachievement or behaviour problems. At the *2008 Canadian Association of Principal's National Conference* I had the opportunity to gain knowledge of the inventive ways school staffs are responding to students needs for physicality during their recess and lunch breaks.

It is important to note that these educational leaders clearly grasp that a pedagogy specific to the teaching boys as a homogeneous group is precarious territory, but still acknowledge that biological and cultural tendencies between genders have been shown to exist. They agreed that boys do not need excuses for bad behaviour, nor do they need rescue from their masculinity. While all boys need respect, discipline, and understanding, high-spirited boys additionally need the opportunity to engage in rough-and-tumble play at recess and lunch that is safe and respectful. These adults recognize that keeping these boys inside during breaks for earlier infractions is simply foolhardy.

School principals everywhere observe that when many boys—and some girls—are freshly sprung from the immobility some classrooms present, they can become raucous, rowdy and rambunctious during breaks. They also know that these boys prefer to play in large groups, in a constant struggle for one-upmanship as the leader of the pack emerges, within game structures that are vigourous, intense, and focussed on scores. These boys want to win.

Three examples of the principals' insight into action include: Wrestling, Reverse Lunch, and the *Hockey Box Recess.*

Wrestling

Why is it that boys get into trouble for playing games like *King of the Mountain, Dodge Ball,* throwing snowballs or wrestling? Some parents complain that even tag has been banned on the playground because it violates a school's no-touching policy.

Experts proclaim that rough-and-tumble play characterized by running, chasing, fleeing, playful fighting and wrestling is essential to the development of self-confidence and is a critical part of boys' healthy development. Most note that this type of play is very different from aggression. In rough-and-tumble play, children enjoy themselves, there is a lot of laughing, and the participants part as friends. In aggression, there is no laughter, children are often hurt, and they part as enemies.

School principals of both genders are successfully engaging in action research projects that emphasize ways to channel the bounce in raucous boys and are taking the time to teach them reasonable limits to play wrestle. These leaders are convinced that establishing routines for structuring wrestling just might also lead to fewer behaviour problems during the break and even increased learning between breaks. One female principal asserted that there was an additional consideration warranting attention with respect to physicality and recess and offered her own mother's wisdom as a school principal many years ago: "If they're not dirty, they didn't have fun. Remember that kids are kids and dirt is not the enemy."

Reverse Lunch

For those of you who are not yet familiar with a reverse lunch schedule, it involves going outside to play first and eating afterwards. The support is growing for reversing these activities from teachers, parents and researchers alike. Ask elementary youth and they will tell you that one of the best parts of their day is lunchtime. Not because of nutritional sustenance but because they get to play with their friends. Children—boys especially—are often too excited to eat; they just can't wait to get outside. The ingrained school ritual of eating first and playing later is being challenged to channel children's need for physical activity, increase student nutrition, and hopefully their scholastic performance.

Hockey Box Recess

When I first heard about **Herbert Spencer Elementary's** *Hockey Box Recess* for Grade 1 students in New Westminster, BC, I was compelled to observe firsthand. As I sat awaiting the break, it seemed as though the young boys realized recess was near as they nodded silently toward the clock. To what degree did these boys actually know how to read a clock or whether they were engaged in a very subtle form of communication is a topic for another time.

When the bell rang they collectively sprang to attention and proficiently lined up to select a hockey stick just outside their classroom door. I smiled as they each took vigilant attention to hold the stick in a very specific way, ensuring safety as they made their way toward the playground exit door. It struck me that they appeared as a marching band, navigating the school hallways where children from other classrooms were also making their way to celebrate recess. Once outside they raced to the middle of the playground where a chain linked fence provided a secure space to play hockey, about half the size of a typical classroom. I am told that while girls were welcome to participate they rarely elected to play. These boys discovered endless bundles of energy as they played hockey with all their hearts.

I observed no high checking or body checking. They clearly knew the rules of engagement. Only once did I observe a potential problem erupt with two sticks colliding during an intense scrimmage resulting in one boy dropping his stick. I realized that our beloved **NHL** had instilled in me the expectation that a squirmish was sure to erupt, but instead after these two boys' eyes met they simultaneously broke eye contact and both looked outside the *Hockey Box* to where a playground supervisor smiled, nodding that they should resume play. They hardly skipped a beat and played until exhaustion and the recess period bell rang. In that instant I was reminded that it is the certainty not the severity of the consequence that counts. I had learned that the staff had taken ample time for training and followed through on their promise of providing supervision.

Weather Forecast: Sunny and Blue — Recess Sky Approaching

Many parents and teachers will be pleased to learn that the storm associated with keeping students inside during recess rather than sending them outside to play may be passing. Last month a first-of-its-kind national **Gallup** poll of almost 2000 school principals reported overwhelmingly that recess has a strong positive impact on academic achievement, that students listened better and were more focussed after recess, and that student's social development and well-being also improved. These school principals likely recognize that when children are freshly sprung from mainly sedentary classrooms, they can work off their nervous rambunctious energy without disrupting classroom activities. These leaders no doubt have long recognized how counter-productive it is to keep boys inside during breaks because of earlier infractions.

Recess is not a privilege to be taken away when boys get distracted or act out in class. Recess is a basic right.

Recess primes the pump for academic learning, and promotes child development in a variety of ways. Recess is as critical as the *Three R's*—Reading, Writing, and Arithmetic. In fact, with continued support from engaged parents and teachers, reces just might become the *Fourth R.*

20　Should Recess be Withdrawn for Incomplete Schoolwork?

WHILE most parents and teachers agree that the free play afforded during recess has many benefits, especially for boys who need to recharge their batteries by moving, a strongly worded comment from a teacher reveals discomfort with the idea of recess as a basic right.

The Truth About Consequences

Dear Barry,

I had the good fortune of attending your presentation in Ottawa and have since been sharing your newsletters with colleagues. I often appreciate your perspective, but have some concerns regarding the *Recess Matters!* article.

As you read my concerns, keep in mind that the average student in my class does not act up or fail to complete class work on a regular basis and the vast majority of my students are not kept in at recess.

I am concerned with the parent's analogy that "we require our workplaces to give a break to adults, so why would we not require the same for our kids?" and your later comment about recess being a basic right. Don't we teach children that along with rights come responsibilities? If a child spends 20 or 40 minutes playing, cutting loose, and doing their own thing during class time, do they need another 20 to 40 minutes to play, cut loose and do their own thing outside at recess or lunch?

I agree with your claim that providing more time to learn does not ensure that more learning will take place, but I wonder why you would not support keeping a child in from recess when the child is not assuming the responsibility to learn during classroom time.

What if I told you that when students goof off in my class, I've seen a lot of learning take place in the last ten minutes of class when I remind students that the work I assigned must be completed, or else they get no recess?

I think it is interesting that the parent's focus is primarily "My son has rights and teachers should not be allowed to infringe on his rights." Shouldn't this parent ask: "What can I do to help my child become a more productive learner?"

Kevin

Dear Kevin,

I agree that the association between rights and responsibilities is a valuable part of our social contract. When rights are demanded and responsibilities are avoided, children are more likely to become self-absorbed and even helpless. Accentuating rights without attending to responsibilities can lead to many problems, including an inflated sense of self-importance, an excessive need for admiration.

However, I might also add that the capacity to link cause and effect is something that comes with time, as our brains develop. It is the frontal lobe of the brain that gives us capacity to make this link, and it is the last part of our brains to mature. The slow development of this crucial cognitive ability explains why young people can at times perceive that they are invincible; that they can goof off in class, as the teacher won't catch them; that they can delay completing an important assignment, as it is not due for a week; that certain social behaviours will damage reputations, but not theirs; that some drugs are addictive, but not for them.

As children grow toward adulthood, they will develop a stronger sense of the link between rights and responsibilities, but we must be cautious not to compare children to adults when it comes to balancing the two. As we set forth our expectations, we must consider the amount of liability that young people are capable of assuming.

Of course, growth and development are not lock-step. Even the most supportive and skilled adults will at times find themselves stymied by a boy's inconsistent and unpredictable behaviour. You are wise to suggest that parents ought to inquire with a teacher about how they might support their child's learning.

In turn, you will likely agree that teachers ought to also keep parents informed when unfavourable learning patterns emerge—such as not submitting assignments or acting up in class. Rather than simply assuming the problem is the student's or the parent's, the teacher may help by providing parents with a corresponding educational plan. Educators who are also parents often convey to me their frustrations on both sides of this quandary. As a classroom teacher, I certainly recall disappointment when parents did not appear to support their child's learning, but as a parent I also became annoyed when teachers expected me alone to remedy a problem—especially when someone else had established unrealistic expectation, such as assigning excessive homework over spring break!

Withdrawing Recess May Feed Resentment Toward Learning

As outlined in the previous newsletter *Recess Matters!*, many parents, teachers, administrators, and researchers do not support the idea of keeping a child in at recess or lunchtime to complete classroom work or to remedy misbehaviour. Over the past month I received dozens of emails from parents expressing their concern about withholding recess and lunch playtime. Many emphasize that the imposition of this sanction simply fuels increased frustration and anger toward classroom learning. One email from a Calgary parent stands out in particular:

> Keeping my son in during recess on a regular basis has never helped him in the past. Why would a teacher assume that it's going to help now? When my son has to remain inside at recess, I do not believe that he is thinking 'Gee, now I understand why I need to cooperate more in class!' I wish your article

would have paid more attention to what students are asked to do in class, as I am also concerned that while the teacher is labelling my son as the problem by keeping him in at recess, the teacher is not questioning how he might have created conditions that contributed to the disturbance. As a medical doctor by profession, I am unable to separate a person's health from their environmental context. Isn't the classroom curriculum and culture part of the larger context that my son is responding to? I do know that when my son's curiosity is piqued and he is presented with creative opportunities to stretch his thinking, he truly wants to reflect on his learning and complete assignments—especially thoughtful, meaningful assignments that allow him to demonstrate his unique approach to learning.

Emails from many frustrated parents indicate that month-after-month which turn into year-after-year, punitive sanctions do not work. "We need to stop labelling and pathologizing boys," says a father in another email. "We need to stop talking about them in disapproving language, as if the vast majority of them are living with some intractable disability. It is the system that needs to change."

Many parents worry that their son's frustrations and unmet learning needs will be driven underground to incubate and smoulder. Parents also worry that their son's resentment will flare up later at school and elsewhere, manifesting as defiance, anger, and disengagement.

While I appreciate that the majority of children in your classroom are not held in at recess or lunchtime to complete assignments, I do have reservations about the motivational strategy of informing students that their work must be completed or their recess will be withheld.

Often, when we adults use the term *motivation*, we really mean *compliance*. Naturally, we want to see children do what we tell them to do, and we may be tempted to use manipulative strategies to get children to comply with our wishes. Those of us raised on punitive approaches to child-rearing are more likely to conclude that we can motivate children to perform better and achieve more through a system of external rewards and punishments. However, parents who have tried to improve their children's performance by giving cash for grades, or sanctions such as grounding, usually come to recognize the limitations of these strategies. Parents who have shared with me stories of their own forays into the exchange economy of *Do this and I'll give you that* have observed that rewards can also flip into punishment. Cash for grade depends on satisfying the parent, and when the going gets tough, a child's focus on the far-off prize may shift to an awareness of being controlled. The frustration associated with the withheld cash then seems like a punishment. And the more desirable the reward, the more demoralizing it is to miss out.

Most teachers and parents also come to recognize that disciplinary approaches based on coercion, threats, and punishments do little to help youth to internalize self-discipline and self-motivation. External manipulations may at times appear to work for a short time, but they do not, in the long run, teach children to become caring, responsible, and ethical people who will act appropriately without external supervision or coercion. Strategies of external manipulation may even backfire, as children learn to become master manipulators themselves—some people reading this might recall how the two-faced Eddie Haskell on the 1950's sitcom *Leave It to Beaver* could act one way around adults, and quite another way when they were not around.

Forcing Compliance Is Not the Same as Meeting a Boy's Needs

Years of working with underachieving boys have taught me first-hand about the limitations of *motivating* them through the use of external control devices. We all can appreciate that a tired, scared, and frustrated boy in Grade 7 will agree to almost any behaviour intervention plan in the heat of the moment during a behaviour support meeting. He will likely even sign the behavioural contract presented to him just to end the heated anxiety he feels as he sits with the adults assembled, but inwardly these boys later reveal to me that they view such meetings and the signing of contracts as a sham. These boys often tell me that their classes are dull, uninspiring, and that failure seems to be a built in expectation. Sometimes I can see that they are trying to slither out of responsibility and shift blame, as frustrated adolescents are prone to do, but more often than not, I have seen how the ways their learning needs are left undefined and unaddressed.

As most parents reading this article will have limited experience with a school behaviour intervention meeting, I do want to clarify that about fifty percent of the time these meetings do uncover core issues and generate positive outcomes, but I believe that we can do better. What troubles me the most about unsuccessful *collaborative meetings* is that they identify students as problems and focus on symptomatic behaviours, not the whole person. The aim is not usually to seek out how adults might better capitalize on strengths or address unmet learning needs; instead it is to figure out how the child can be made to do what adults want him to do. We tell ourselves that our focus on extracting compliance is for the student's own good.

However, in my experience, a student who disappoints is missing something critical, something he needs, something he cannot put into words—and something that I believe it is our job, as educators, to try to learn about.

Last year, I recall attending a behaviour support meeting at a school where the classroom teacher and the district support behaviour teacher determined that the central problem facing a particular boy was that he needed to remain in his seat more frequently; as by getting up and moving around the classroom, he was interrupting the learning of others and himself. As I listened to the mounting evidence, it seemed that when the boy's inability to stay seated was being read as the real problem, a seeming solution could be positive reinforcement tactics that would train the boy to remain in his seat. Presumably the boy would become satisfied with the rewards he would receive as compensation. The discussion did not, however, factor in the boy's perspective, or the boy's recent diagnosis of *Obsessive Compulsive Disorder* and *Attention Deficit Hyperactivity Disorder.* Getting up and out of his seat was the least of his problems! I also suspect that wandering around the classroom was his unskillful attempt to manage his struggles with OCD and ADHD. This boy had serious anxiety issues that were misunderstood.

Coercing and manipulating boys to follow our agendas, without regard for motive or context or underlying emotions, does not work.

Several years ago I was employed as a district coordinator for students at risk of underachieving. I repeatedly observed that for those boys who were labelled as recalcitrant, their troubles in their school careers could typically be traced back to ineffective sanctions, such as regular lunchtime and recess detentions.

When we employ intervention strategies, we educators must ask:

Are we doing this to try to help the boy or to make our lives easier?

Are we doing something to the boy, or are we working with him in a respectful and authentic collaboration?

I have often noticed the curious pattern of adults concluding behavioural meetings with comments like, "Now, it's up to you, Johnny. You have the power to choose cooperation or you can choose the consequence." When we posit such choices, are we telling the truth? If the choice is between complying with our wishes or missing out on something of value, is that a real choice? Although very young children can usually only manage two choices at once, by the time children reach primary school, most can generate several possibilities. Doesn't wrapping a threat in the language of choice falsely pretend there is volition to decide? How confusing it must be for the child who genuinely struggles with learning and relationships to be told: "You chose this consequence yourself." Could this be a game of adult posturing such as 'heads I win, tails you lose'?

Recently, I overhead a teacher explain to a parent: "We can't help your son if he doesn't help himself." But do children who legitimately struggle with authentic life problems really have the power to override their unskilled compensatory strategies to protect themselves; to cover up trauma; to conceal shame; to mask unmet needs?

As the famous child psychologist, Virginia Axline, author of *Play Therapy*, once said: "All people proceed with a caution that will protect the integrity of their personality."

I know that at times some children may be very deliberate as they manoeuvre their teacher so that they will end up spending recess and lunchtime at their desk or in the hallway. Just last week, I observed a 12 year old boy grin broadly after receiving a *consequence*, indicating that he would rather be in the hallway or at the office rather than sitting in a classroom where he was bored, frustrated, and alienated. About a month ago another boy explained to me how satisfying it was to be suspended from school for telling his teacher to *F—off* during class and in front of peers because, he explained: "I got to give him some of his own medicine." Even if this child's inappropriate language was deliberate manipulation, we have to wonder about the underlying reasons he would choose isolation over the social connection and belonging that is such a fundamental human need.

Do we really believe that children misbehave on purpose or that they choose to stay inside at recess while others socialize and play?

Looking at Underlying Patterns of Behaviour

I would suggest that before we rush to threaten to withhold recess or apply some other sanction, we ought first ask ourselves broader and deeper questions:

- Is there a pattern to the misbehaviour or underachievement? If so, what might the pattern reveal?

- What might a particular boy be saying through his behaviour that we have not understood?

- How might we look beyond his recalcitrant behaviour to better understand what he needs?

- If the boy is old enough, who might respectfully seek his input and invite him into authentic partnership? How could we work collaboratively to a positive outcome that he can be part of?

As we dig deeper to understand a particular boy's needs, we might recall that children naturally want to learn. You don't have to bribe a young child to show you how to put together a new toy or decode the rules of a new video game. One of the most thoroughly researched findings in social psychology is that the more you reward someone for doing something, the less interest that person will tend to have in whatever he or she was rewarded to do. Yet, research also shows that by about Grade 4 or 5, the inquiring minds and intrinsic motivation of many boys starts to trail off sharply, just around the time that grades are introduced. How can we tune into children's innate curiosity and engage with children where they are?

Most of us can remember times when we really connected with a teacher, how learning was a real pleasure and the acquisition of new skills seemed almost effortless. Maybe there were even moments when we were so absorbed in what we were discovering that we had no sense of time passing. We may also remember dead times of disconnection—from the teacher, from the environment, from our bodies, and from the learning task that seemed so remote from anything we valued.

As educators or as parents, we want our children to be connected and alive. Understanding varied learning needs can shed light on diverse learning pathways for headstrong and disruptive boys.

Different Approaches for Different Learners

The four questions below can spur reflection on different learning styles and needs.

1. Is he a visual learner struggling in a verbal classroom?

Where verbal learners get more out of words and written and spoken explanations, visual learners remember best what they see: pictures, diagrams, flow charts, time lines, films, and demonstrations.

2. Is he an active learner surrounded primarily by reflective learning designs?

Where reflective learners prefer to think about what they are learning quietly first, active learners retain and understand information best by doing something active. "Let's try it out and see how it works," the active learner proclaims. "Let's think it through first," the reflective learner responds.

3. Is he an intuitive learner who struggles with detailed memorization and routine calculations?

Detail learners patiently and carefully gather particulars and learn the facts; intuitive learners prefer abundant, disorganized details where they may spot possibilities and relationships.

4. Is he a macro learner who struggles with micro-logical and sequential paths to finding solutions?

Micro learners gain understanding in linear steps, with each step following logically from the previous one. Macro learners learn in large jumps, absorbing material almost randomly without seeing connections, and then suddenly getting it.

In addition to considering individual learning needs, we can take time to teach children and adolescents how to get along and thrive in communities. We might:

1. Encourage students to learn appropriate behaviour among themselves, with the teacher's guidance. Have classroom discussions about the standards of behaviour that don't just lay out prescribed rules such as the school's code of conduct, but also provide students with opportunities to explore and determine how to genuinely work and learn together as a collaborative community.

2. Establish routine classroom meetings where students are able to vent their frustration, discuss classroom issues and learn how to solve problems in a democratic setting. They might even call into question excessive homework or punitive sanctions.

3. Foster safe and caring learning environments that nurture inclusive participation from all students, without fear of mockery, degradation or putdowns.

Children deserve an engaging curriculum and a caring atmosphere so they can act on their natural desire to learn and grow their talents. Even when students make poor choices, we can challenge outmoded aspects of our education system designed to create unthinking and compliant students. Children do not deserve to be manipulated with extrinsic controls. As many studies have shown, extrinsic rewards and punishments are not simply ineffective over time; they are actually counter-productive, supplanting the innate desire to learn that is part of our human nature.

At times we look out from the wrong end of the telescope. Fostering real and lasting change in a discouraged child necessitates a better understanding of what *motivates* the child, not just how we can motivate him.

May we, as educators and parents, do more than tinker with strategies of compliance.

May we learn to attune with care to the many different needs of our youth, supporting and inspiring meaningful change in their lives—and in the lives of our learning communities.

21 Questioning Zero Tolerance & School Suspension

What are the real costs of the suspended student's further disconnectedness from school?

AS parents and educators, we naturally want to know that schools are safe, secure places where our children can thrive. When we hear about lock-downs, school shootings, bullying, or other credible threats to our students' safety, we may long for swift, certain and decisive responses that will guarantee our children's well-being.

Students, parents and staff need to trust that endangerment of those in our care will not be permitted at school.

I agree that there should be a clear-cut and swift response to those truly threatening—but rare—behaviours such as gun or knife possession. However, many thoughtful educators question the effectiveness of a heavy-handed application of a *Zero Tolerance* policy, where the law is used as a weapon of control for common misbehaviours. What are the logical consequences of using suspension and expulsion every time the school's conduct code is violated? Who is learning what when suspension is the knee-jerk disciplinary response to a range of typical adolescent misbehaviours such as swearing, defiance, smoking and even truancy?

It is worthy of note that even among recent national reports reviewing literature on school safety, including the **U.S. Surgeon General's Report** on *Youth Violence*, none has designated *Zero Tolerance* or suspension as an effective or even as a promising approach. Put more simply, there is no data that *Zero Tolerance* or suspension makes a difference either in improving school safety or improving student behaviour.

We might also ask ourselves why boys at a certain age return from the office or from a suspension to a hero's welcome.

How logical is the idea that a student who skips school should be punished by not being allowed to come to school? How fair is it to impose a suspension that is lengthier than the time missed?

Student success initiatives address underlying causes of misbehaviour and underachievement rather than punishing students by sending them home, particularly for truancy, tardiness and disengagement.

According to sociologist Karen Sterneimer, we may choose to focus on schools as scary places in order to avoid looking at systematic problems facing the schools—problems of overcrowding, tired and obsolescent materials, fragmented communities. It is certainly easier to see troubled students and misbehaviour as the problem, rather than raising questions about larger institutional issues, or about the underlying reasons for student disengagement, apathy, or even aggression.

In my work with youth, parents and teachers over the years, I have consistently found that truant and tardy students are often anxious and frustrated students. These youth, who are typically overwhelmed with managing school and life responsibilities, need support, not admonishment. Evidence shows children are more likely to grow into caring, courageous and ethical people when they are treated with respect rather than manipulative control.

The following email from a parent raises questions about the effectiveness of suspension and *Zero Tolerance* as applied to a misbehaviour fairly typical for adolescents on a school fieldtrip. It also highlights how consequences should be carefully designed so that they do not inadvertently become reinforcers.

Dear Barry,

Recently our son was suspended from school. My husband and I have consistently backed up school staff over the years, but this time their decision to suspend seems harsh and just wrong. Allow me to elaborate.

Our son James who is in Grade 11, travelled to a neighbouring town on the weekend with his boys' basketball team for the regional games. The girls' team also travelled to the same town for the same purpose, and each team stayed at hotels across the street from each other. Before departure the youth were told that the two teams were not to have any contact whatsoever and that breaking this rule would result in immediate withdrawal of play and school suspension.

As it turned out, my son and two other boys broke the rule and visited their girlfriends at the girls' hotel lobby on Friday night around 10pm. Apparently when the teacher chaperone approached the lobby my son and his friend hid in the lobby washroom while the third boy ran down a hallway and into one of the girl's rooms.

In response to the girls' nervous gestures and giggling the chaperone suspected something was up and pressed the girls for information. They avoided the truth, but rumour has it that one of the girls kept looking at the male lobby washroom. The jig was up and everyone was caught.

As an example to the other team players all three boys and five girls involved were withdrawn from all of the weekend games and the boys received an official one day suspension from school upon return. The boy who ran down the hallway and into one of the girl's hotel room received a three-day suspension. Upon returning to school after a day at home the school staff gave the impression that because the piper had been paid the discipline was now over.

When I questioned the principal about the appropriateness of the withdrawal of play and suspension he said: "It was the rule. They broke the rule. Now they must pay the price. Don't worry, all will be well in a couple of days." I walked away incensed with his simplistic thinking and the lack of appreciation for what it's like to be 16.

The youth involved are very angry about not playing basketball and being suspended and it seems that our community of parents are conducting informal parking lot polls and taking sides. While some expected it to happen others tout on about tough love. Is the school's method of managing behaviour appropriate in this situation? What should I do?

Wilma

Dear Wilma,

Watching our children grow toward independence can be both a heartwarming and heartrending experience.

When kids get off-track in some way, parents are often told that teaching responsibility requires laying down the law, as well as demanding compliance with increasingly strict rules. Yet, as any parent of an adolescent knows, it's a lot easier to make the rules than to enforce—or negotiate—them.

Before considering any disciplinary action, we need ask ourselves: "What's the task?" Is it reasonable to expect that young males and females in Grade 11 not visit each other while on a parallel sport's fieldtrip?

Your school's rule about *no opposite gender peer contact on trips* reminds me of the simplistic tactics counselled by *Supernanny* or *Assertive Discipline*, where everything—including young people's feelings and critical reflections—are sacrificed to the imperative of obedience. Black and white rules, with unswerving enforcement, may work with canine training, but have limited effectiveness with youth.

Television's no-nonsense *Supernanny* who orders that kids stand in the *naughty corner* would likely support your school administrator's decision to suspend, but I have grim reservations about the effectiveness of suspensions, as well as what is commonly referred to as a *Zero Tolerance* approach to teach youth appropriate behaviour. At its core *Zero Tolerance* relies on bribes and threats with the underlying purpose of enforcement. But what if the school's rules do not reflect best practice? What if the rules are a set-up for failure? What if these rules have been designed simply to **get the trains to run on time**—not minding whom they run over?

Why Zero Tolerance and School Suspension are Counterproductive

Zero Tolerance is counter-productive because it doesn't teach respect or cooperation. No one is born with perfect social skills. Don't we need to model the respect and kindness we want to see in adolescents?

Suspension is a controversial school practice. Being suspended often reduces the student's sense of connectedness to school, so that the youth have less and less to lose. It can also be counter-productive when a boy who bucks the system receives a hero's welcome upon return. Are staff and administrators at your school aware of the studies that question the limited effectiveness of school suspension? Are they aware of measures they can take to reduce the use of school suspensions, and the current research about the benefits of restorative discipline?

When young people are forced to obey rules that to them seem arbitrary, they often feel disrespected, and then have to figure out some way to shore up their personal integrity. Depending upon how powerful they feel or what options they see as open to them, they may fight openly, or they may resist passively. **Laying down the law** teaches that **might makes right,** and that respect goes in only one direction—up!

It is natural for boy-girl interaction to occur on a field trip. This occasion could provide parents and teachers opportunities to provide mentorship, a chance to discuss hormones, attractions and self-guidance. They might even arrange co-ed chaperoned meetings or activities while young people are away from home.

Inviting Youth into Authentic Dialogue

Responding to the predictable ups and downs of teenage experimentation is less about managing or controlling behaviour, and more about promoting dialogue, reflection and responsibility. Engaging in authentic conversation with teens means learning to let go of some control, some part of the adult agenda. Adults must learn to listen to young people as they engage in the potentially awkward and unpredictable process of working with youth to decide what socially responsible behaviour looks like. This doesn't mean that youth automatically get their way. They do, however, need their say.

Learning to set up discipline that teaches takes time, patience and skill. However, evidence shows children are more likely to grow into caring, courageous and ethical people when they are treated with calm reason and the warmth of empathy rather than the tools of *Darth Vader-like* control.

I encourage you to discuss my comments and suggestions with your school administrator. Remember too that your school principal may have pieces to the puzzle that you are not aware of or rationales that you have not considered. If you are met with defensiveness, provide some time and space for reflection and revisit the discussion a few days later.

If you think that your school administrator is open, you might consider mentioning *Boy Smarts: Mentoring Boys for Success at School*—chapter 9, *Discipline that Teaches Rather than Punishes*—and also collaboration 9 in Boy *Smarts Action Study Guide,* which deals with restorative measures and alternatives to suspension.

Another useful resource for school administrators is the **British Columbia Ministry of Education** document *Focus on Suspension: A Resource for Schools* (1999), which was made available to all BC school administrators and encourages educators to develop alternatives to suspension: "Suspension may in some situations have no effect or even increase the likelihood of the behaviour reoccurring…. out-of-school suspensions can contribute to a student's alienation from school and the likelihood of the student dropping out."

Although a few school administrators hand out suspensions easily, most school principals recognize their limitations, and even their counter-productiveness. These wise principals, who know that the unflinching enforcement of rules does not create inner responsibility or pro-social behaviour, reach for more creative responses to young people's behavioural challenges. They know well that students learn respect for self and others through supportive school climates, respectful interventions when necessary, and skilled, empathic guidance of the next generation.

22   When Sitting Still Is Not Enough

AT one time in traditional schools, teachers were rewarded for classrooms filled with the sounds of silence and stillness. Some students learned to perform the act of attention, but sitting with head bowed did not always mean that they were learning. Now we know that learning involves the body as well as the mind, and that kinesthetic learners in particular learn best when they can use movement. Creative teachers can capitalize on some students' high energy levels by seeing energy as a resource, and helping to channel it in appropriate, and sometimes helpful ways. Students will develop more connection to their own needs and more internal self-control and monitor their own impulses if they are given simple supports such as *Take a Break* cards, described below.

Building Resilience for Active Learners

Dear Barry,

Even before my son Logan started school, I was aware that his activity levels would challenge most adults he encountered. Logan fidgets, struggles to sit still, and becomes easily distracted by anything that moves or makes a sound. When something is bothering him, he prefers to hop on a bike rather than sit at a table and talk. He has no desire to read step-by-step instructions on assembling a new toy, but will, for better or worse, delve right in.

Logan isn't a visual learner who thinks in pictures, reading a teacher's body language and facial expressions in order to fully understand the content of a lesson.

Logan is also not an auditory learner, preferring to listen to verbal instructions and talk things through while considering what others have to say.

Logan needs physical action. He is a kinesthetic learner who needs to move, do, and touch whatever he is learning.

As a primary student, Logan would frequently get into trouble for cutting up erasers and paper, shredding whatever he could find to keep himself busy. I struggled to help him find his way without my interventions, but it was obvious to me that teachers needed to adapt traditional approaches to classroom learning if they were to meet Logan's kinesthetic needs.

As a special education teacher and a mother of a son diagnosed with ADHD, I completely agree with the *Boy Smarts* assertion that many BOYS NEED MOVEMENT. I am particularly sensitive to the pressures on parents to seek a medical diagnosis for what is considered hyperactivity and then to medicate their child. I am aware of the potential side effects of ADHD drugs and know that drug intervention for highly distractible students is viewed differently around the world; that approximately ninety percent of the world's *Ritalin* is prescribed in the United States.

I recognize that a small percentage of students may indeed benefit with drug intervention that can help them to focus, learn, and develop much needed confidence. But educators and parents are not qualified to discuss drug interventions for ADHD or ADD, and I believe that it is shortsighted to rush to medicate children. What are some drug-free strategies that we teachers can use to support kids who are more distractible and kinesthetic?

Rita

Dear Rita,

When boys are striking out, it is essential that parents be consulted as partners. Parents and teachers may look at children's learning from different perspectives, but they share a common goal—making sure that children receive the best education possible. Communication between home and school takes advantage of both perspectives to provide children with the kind of care and education that will help them thrive.

Different Interventions for Different Children

Consider the following checklist of questions for parents and teachers to collaboratively determine what will work best for a particular child:

1.   What are non-distracting ways that students can be active while working at their desks?

Do students have active-sitting devices, allowing for gentle and quiet side-to-side movements at their desks, perhaps working; a large ball, a small inflatable cushion, or even a single-legged stool?

Are students permitted to stand while working at their desks?

2.   Are students permitted fidget toys—squeeze balls, erasers, wooden beads—to keep in their pockets and use quietly as needed? Are students encouraged to doodle constructively to improve their attention level?

3.   Where is the student sitting in the classroom?

Is he seated near high traffic areas, or near the least distracting location in the classroom?

Does he find it calming to sit near the teacher, or does this location seem punitive?

Is it helpful to surround the student with constructive role models?

4.   Is the student's seating placement isolating, or does it seem integrated in a natural way in the classroom? Certainly sending students into the hall can communicate to other students that he does not belong.

5. How does the child respond when given the opportunity to move back and forth between two seating locations in the classroom throughout the day—

perhaps one location with a group of other students, and another quieter and less-distracting location?

How can he be empowered so that the alternative location is a choice, not a punishment?

6.   Might playing soft music—without lyrics—in the classroom help to reduce background distractions made by fans inside or machines outside the classroom?

7.   How frequently are movement breaks built into the classroom routines?

Where can students independently move to in the classroom without distracting others?

8.   Are kinesthetic learners ever held in at recess or lunchtime when they need the activity most?

Regardless of classroom misbehaviour, are active learners allowed to go outside at recess to blow off steam and participate in physical activities?

Do you notice that these students are more attentive and productive after they run off excess energy and restlessness?

If they return to the class and struggle with settling down, what transitions might be used to help them refocus to the learning activity?

9.   When transitions are difficult for some students, is it helpful to give advance warning that a transition is about to take place?

How do students react to other transition cues, such as dimming lights, playing music, or finding novel ways to signal an activity change?

Which students benefit when they are prompted about the transition before the rest of the class?

Is it possible to integrate a transition activity that helps others, perhaps going to the library, gym, or buddy class a few minutes early to ensure that the next teacher is notified that class will arrive soon?

How might a particular student respond if he is invited to exit a minute or two early to complete a task that helps others, such as posting a sign on the adventure playground about which students get to use the equipment that day?

How can classroom routines be organized so that students who have difficulty handling the stimulation of exiting for recess or lunchtime with the rest of the class receive additional transition time?

10.   How does the active learner respond to doing errands in the classroom, such as passing out papers or putting materials away, so they have legitimate options to move about the classroom in appropriate and helpful ways?

11.   Are students permitted the option to *Take a Break* when then need one?

For example, after notifying their teacher, the student may leave the classroom and present a *Take a Break* card to librarian or the resource room teacher. The student then spends the next five minutes engaging in a prearranged activity such as working on a puzzle or looking at a favourite book. When the time is up, the supervising adult thanks the student for visiting and instructs the student to return to their classroom. Note that the *Take a Break* strategy addresses a student's genuine need for movement and should not be linked to misbehaviour.

The *Take a Break* strategy can also be expanded to help students plan their breaks throughout the day. For example, the student might begin the day with a set number of *Take a Break* cards and be responsible for planning how they will use them throughout the day.

12.   To what degree are students given opportunities to use active responses as part of instructional activities? For example, students may turn and talk with a partner, stand up to indicate agreement, or move to different parts of the room to use materials.

Are students permitted to work at different stations such as at a large table, the board, an easel, or chart paper on a wall?

While the questions here do not address all dimensions of kinesthetic learners, it is my hope that they will uncover how the rhythm of the school day structure can help and hinder the easily distractible and kinesthetic student. Collaborative inquiry between parent and teacher will foster understanding about the needs of a particular high-spirited learner and identify ways to channel his rambunctious energy in constructive ways.

23   Reframing Attitudes Toward Active Learners

How can we shift from irritation to a more compassionate and helpful way with active learners?

WHILE it's natural for teachers to want students to be focussed and attentive at all times, a student who is fidgeting, twisting a tiny rubber elastic figure in his hands, shuffling books noisily, or even gazing absently out the window, has much to teach. Such students are giving cues that something else is needed. It is adult perspectives that will make all the difference in how well these students learn, and how they feel about themselves.

Typically, it is around reporting time that teachers tell me about the pressures of preparing report cards and how they can more easily become frustrated with challenging behaviours at school. One teacher recently emailed about her own frustration and her own attitude *makeover*:

Dear Barry,

Like clockwork, preparing report cards increases my tension on the job. Even my own kids and husband notice my stress level building. This year my son innocently announced that I needed a *makeover* or else he'd move out. Sensing the mounting tension among my colleagues, I know that I am not alone. I am a bit of a perfectionist and want to do my best to inform parents about their children's achievement. It can be hard at times not to spiral down into discouragement and frustration with

certain student behaviours, especially the short attention spans associated with ADHD. Still, I work hard to maintain optimism and focus on
student strengths.

As you emphasize in each of your *Boy Smarts* stories, I too have discovered that when I shift my focus to student strengths and work to see the
silver-lining of challenging behaviours, students learn that I care about
them and respect their unique ways of learning. When I look from a place
of compassion, we both discover more patience—and I get my reports
cards done on time! I recall a list of *mindset makeover* you summarized at a conference that I found to be helpful and inspiring, and
would appreciate the list again. Thank you!"

Shelley

Dear Shelley,

As you attend to the challenging task of teaching the youth of today you are
wise to focus on their strengths, appreciating that being a little different can
be advantageous. Studies suggest that many of the traits students with ADHD
exhibit can be expressions of deeper talents: powerful imagination, searching
insight, and unusual intuition. Consider the following list of imaginative and
resourceful men who were diagnosed or believed to have lived with ADHD:

- Sir Issac Newton
- Albert Einstein
- Magic Johnson
- Michael Jordan
- Abraham Lincoln
- Nelson Rockefeller
- Henry Ford
- Pablo Picasso
- Wolfgang Amadeus Mozart

- Galileo
- Alexander Graham Bell
- Babe Ruth
- Michael Phelps
- John F. Kennedy
- Walt Disney
- Bill Cosby
- Vincent Van Gogh
- Steven Spielberg

Reframing Automatic Judgments

By reframing our automatic judgments into more compassionate observations, we can develop more satisfying and productive relationships with students. At the end of the day, the week, the term, as pressures mount, we may also, by taking a breath and tilting our perspective, find that we are feeling kinder toward ourselves.

May the following twenty reframing transformations of thought help you maintain a focus on strengths and foster positive responses to the everyday challenges of parenting and teaching children:

Not Respectful / Judgmental	Respectful / Compassionate
• Distractible & can't focus	• Notices everything around them
• Impulsive	• Spontaneous
• Doesn't try	• Has difficulty getting started
• Hyperactive & can't sit still	• Lots of energy and drive
• Talks too much in class	• Very social and relates well to people
• Inappropriate behaviour	• Lacks awareness about behaviour
• Attention-seeker	• Needing contact, support, reassurance
• Is lost in daydreams	• Has tons of creative ideas
• Never finishes things	• Good at starting new projects
• Irritating or annoying	• Challenged—low frustration tolerance
• Stubborn & argumentative	• Independent & knows own mind
• Unwilling	• Unable
• Lazy, unmotivated	• Tired of failing & struggles to begin
• Doesn't care	• Has difficulty sustaining attention
• Reacts & becomes mean	• Becomes defensive, hurt, unhappy
• Refuses to sit still	• Over-stimulated
• Lacks discipline to focus	• Learns quickly through doing
• Resists help & direction	• Is embarrassed & frustrated
• A show-off	• Overcompensates
• Never plans ahead & is impulsive	• Thinks on feet & able to react quickly

Keep in mind those children who struggle with attention, focus, or ADHD challenges often become creative and resourceful learners out of necessity. With maturity, these children develop wonderful traits such as creativity, divergent thinking, inquisitiveness, spontaneity, intuitiveness, resourcefulness, humour, and resilience. As they develop self-confidence in their approach to living, they experience success as adults by choosing careers that build on their unique strengths and abilities. In this way their drive for excitement and stimulation can lead them to success in business, innovation, entertainment, sports and public speaking.

Transformational teachers know that while it's harder to reach some students than others, it's possible to engage almost any student when they tap into their innate interests and strengths to help them learn.

As we hold strong to the conviction that with support, all children can achieve great things, they in turn will learn to channel their energy in positive ways.

24   Appreciating Visual-Spatial Learners

THANKFULLY we now know that learners take in information in a variety of different ways and there are multiple forms of intelligence and each express in creative and differing ways.

What is relatively new on the radar is the appreciation that boys who struggle with achievement, motivation, and even behaviour may be visual-spatial learners who are overwhelmed by the verbosity and wordiness that traditional education holds for them. Fortunately, educators are catching up and offering increased opportunities to learn in visual ways.

How might we respond to visual learners who may flounder in classrooms filled with words?

Dear Barry,

My son is in Grade 7 and does poorly in school. Each year becomes more difficult to get him out the door with this year being the worst. With the exception of problem solving in math and gym class, he complains that learning at school is a waste of time and that he'd rather learn online or play video games.

We carefully monitor his computer time and certainly limit his exposure to shooter-type games. Mostly, we are encouraged to find that he prefers complex thinking games like *World of Warcraft* where he quickly reached the top level and now spends a lot of time coaching other boys to map out their strategies.

When I talk with him to better understand his dislike of school and why he is underachieving he says there is too much talk, not enough action, and he dismisses most writing assignments as boring. While writing his ideas down has never been easy, he can write when he sets his mind to it.

Have we made a mistake by allowing him to play video games? As a younger boy, he always preferred to draw and tell and now I can see that the computer provides him with rich challenges that are so motivating. But what about school?

Monica

Dear Monica,

At one time some educators believed that optimal learning occurred when concepts were introduced in a lock-step manner, practised through drill and repetition, and assessed through written means. Rapid and accurate recall of facts was considered a sign of intelligence; those who excelled at book learning were considered bright and those who learned differently were not. This approach to education did not recognize or value people's varied ways of learning, or what are now referred to as multiple intelligences.

Playing With Ideas in a Visual Dimension

In my wide-ranging discussions with boys, parents and teachers, I have discovered that many boys who dislike conventional learning at school often delight in playing with ideas visually—with *Lego*, puzzles and computer games, for example. These boys may be fascinated with a project blueprint, concentrating on its image at great length, as absorbed as others might be by a captivating novel.

Like DaVinci and Einstein, visual learners who think in pictures may flounder in learning environments that echo with words, words, words. Research has shown that it is common for people who demonstrate above-average talent on the visual-spatial side of their brains to experience some inefficiency with language processing in the left hemisphere of their brains. This inefficiency can take many forms, showing up, for example, as persistent problems with spelling, hesitation with speech, or unusual difficulty with recalling names or with learning foreign languages.

Your son's long-standing attraction to drawing, playing computer games, and working through math problem solving characterize what is called a visual-spatial learning style; visual-spatial learners prefer to organize information and communicate with others through images, pictures, colours, and maps rather than verbally.

They also typically have a first-rate sense of direction and can easily use maps to find their way around. My guess is that when your son walks out of an elevator he has never been on before, he instinctively knows which way to turn.

Visual-spatial learners are capable of rapidly understanding concepts when they can create mental pictures of thoughts and can SEE how ideas are interrelated. It is quite likely that once your son creates a mental picture of an idea and can SEE how the information fits with what he already knows, learning becomes easy for him, and intrinsically motivating.

Over the years I have discovered that visual-spatial learners dislike step-by-step repetition, which they find counter-productive. Once they get a picture of a concept, repeated practice bores them. It's possible when your son is struggling to find a mental picture of something, adults misunderstand his learning process and jump in to remediate with more verbal instruction, more verbal explanation, followed by additional repetition and drill. Often boys like your son get lost as they labor to convert the deluge of words into pictures they can see.

Visual-spatial thinkers may grasp ideas intuitively, almost instantly, without really understanding all aspects of the idea, sometimes even missing steps in logic. Later on visual thinkers like your son may get frustrated with the struggle to convert pictures into words, and then transfer them onto paper. When they become overwhelmed by others' excess verbiage, they may feel inadequate, and give up altogether. Boys your son's age hate to look stupid as they try to find their place. In the classroom these boys tend to appear disorganized. They struggle with deadlines, and do poorly on timed tests. Thus it is not surprising that many of these boys gravitate to the digital world of three-dimensional landscapes filled with moving images. Here, as they rapidly process images and complex problems, they feel smart and in control.

While many visual-spatial learners can develop their oral skills and even tell wonderfully graphic stories and jokes, their written expression often falls short. While we need to keep helping them to develop their writing skills, we also need to recognize that their classroom difficulties are often magnified when they are asked to write the words down.

Sometimes, adults misread visual-spatial learning styles as behavioural, emotional, or learning disabilities. While I don't want to ignore legitimate learning disabilities such as dyslexia, I do wish to emphasize that when we focus on the presenting concern—a struggle with writing—we can miss the deeper issue—a preference for visual-spatial thinking. Understand that when these boys are not visualizing, they are not thinking optimally.

Recently, I learned about a misguided school-based team which sought to have a boy labelled with a severe mental health problem so that he could then receive much more learning support than he currently was receiving with his diagnosis of a written output disorder. The team argued that the boy's increasing display of anxiety in the classroom warranted additional emotional support—counselling for his *low self-esteem*, they claimed. But more support is not always better. We need to be very thoughtful about the particular boy, and his particular needs. The boy in question confided that he disliked getting extra help in the classroom or being pulled out of the class to attend a learning-assistance class. He claimed that when an adult sat beside him in the classroom re-explaining instructions, he felt classmates' judgments and ridicule. It is likely that this perception led to increasing stress, expressed as anxiety.

Learning Strategies for Visual Learners

Rather than battering a boy like this with so-called support of the wrong kind, we need to reflect on how we might offer visual-spatial learners opportunities for learning within the comfort of their visual-spatial preference.

Here are ten very basic suggestions students who think in pictures appreciate:

1. Use mind maps, graphs, systems diagrams, and pictures in place of text.

2. Show films, provide demonstrations, and provide hands-on learning opportunities.

3. Pay attention to colour, layout, and spatial organization of assignments.

4. Provide multiple forms of literacy rich in illustrations and visual imagery.

5. Permit them to present their written work with the assistance of a computer.

6. Do not ask them to copy words from the board.

7. Provide succinct written directions.

8. Provide concise oral instructions that are limited to 2 or 3 steps.

9. Provide reflection opportunities during discussions for students to integrate concepts and create images of concepts.

10. Discuss learning styles in class to ensure that students understand academic difficulties may not be due to personal inadequacies.

Without such adaptations, visual-spatial learners simply become too stressed-out. They may withdraw all interest in school, refusing to write at all, and immerse themselves in the world of computer games where their visual-spatial style of thinking shines.

In response to your question: "Have we made a mistake by allowing him to play video games?" I suggest that you were wise to facilitate your son's love of visual imagery through video games. Recognize that your son's learning style is highly revered in the adult working world. Adults with strong visual-spatial abilities possess the very active mind's eye needed for strategic planning and big-picture thinking, often required of community leaders and company CEO's.

With more and more successful adults acknowledging that moderate gaming develops technological skills needed in their careers you can take additional comfort knowing that a 2007 study published in the *Archives of Surgery* found that surgeons who have a history of playing video games for more than three hours per week may be more accurate than surgeons who have never played video games, with top scorers making forty-seven percent fewer errors in their laparoscopy tests. Some doctors even get ready by playing video games before surgery. The study doesn't support overindulging in video games however and also cautions parents that playing video games alone will not increase the chances of their child getting into medical school.

As a parent you might be tempted to worry that recent brain science discoveries indicate that neuroplasticity—the brain's ability to reorganize itself in response to varied stimulation—likely means that playing more video games has led to your son's increased visual competency and love of video games. You might even imagine that shutting down his participation in a digital universe could encourage his neuroplasticity to develop around his written output. It is not that simple. Generally speaking, these boys are more likely to develop their talents with words when we are able to appreciate the strengths of their visual-spatial style.

It might also be worthwhile noting that Einstein himself said that his most important and productive thinking was done by combinatory play with images in his mind. Not surprisingly, when he was later requested to translate his thought-images into conventional words or the signs of mathematics, he'd complain and laboriously struggle with manipulating his visual pictures into words.

Remember too that many of the brightest minds—those of architects, engineers, designers, sculptors, painters, creative scientists, some mathematicians, as well as computer-graphic artists and game designers—often struggled in word-dominated classrooms, especially in their early years.

Realize that the emerging technology in the world today is a visual technology. Just as Socrates once described the limitations of the emerging technology of his time—books—I can't help but wonder whether, in a word-bound culture, we might be blind to the potentialities and merits of emerging visual technologies associated with computers, blind to the power and imagination of *the mind's eye* which Shakespeare's Hamlet saw so vividly.

Today, teachers understand that everyone has their own unique way of learning, and that the best learning takes place when classroom experiences are enjoyable and relevant to students' lives, interests and experiences.

Computer games, graphics, and visualization technologies are changing the way we experience and process complex information.

Rather than trying to stop this juggernaut, wouldn't we be better off appreciating visual learning styles—and maybe even learning more about understanding, interpreting, and decoding visual images ourselves?

25   Questioning Single-Gender Education

SINGLE-GENDER education has become a hot topic among those who are concerned about boys' struggles in schools. While some tout the merits of this approach, this chapter takes a hard look at this one-size-fits-all response, arguing that the complex social context where learning takes place warrants a more thought out response.

Should we be considering single-gender learning for boys who underachieve?

May 2009

Dear Barry,

In recent years our Ontario educators have been grappling with questions related to closing the significant achievement gap between boys and girls on provincial assessments.

The **Ontario Principals' Council** has recently published an interview with the founder and executive director of the **National Association for Single Sex Public Education** in the United States that has stimulated much discussion about how to raise boys' achievement. While some educators are seriously considering gender-segregated classrooms, others question whether we may be heading into troubled waters by oversimplifying the relationship between gender and learning.

During your keynote address at the **EQAO** conference in Ontario, you challenged educators to consider the diverse learning needs of boys and girls across a broad continuum rather than to simply frame the debate as a binary opposition of boys vs. girls. You maintained that while gender tendencies in learning styles certainly exist, there are more similarities than differences between boys and girls. You argued that the learning needs of children would best be served by improving our understanding of diverse learning needs in our communities rather than dividing learners into two groups—boys and girls.

I am curious what you think about whether the movement toward single-sex education is worthy of pursuit. What are some alternatives that you might suggest we explore?

Joe Lamoureux

President, Ontario Teachers' Federation

Dear Joe,

In many parts of the world there is much discussion around the different educational experiences and eventual learning outcomes for boys and girls. A few decades ago this interest was primarily fuelled by the perception that girls were underachieving in math, and more recently the focus has shifted to boys' lagging scores in reading and writing.

Discussion of the relationship between gender and learning can sometimes create more heat than light in our school communities. When we read worrying statistics about the achievement gap between boys and girls in many parts of the world, our sense of alarm may tempt us to grab onto trendy ideas that appear promising. In our darker moments, we may wonder whether anything can be done with boys who are bored, disconnected, and underachieving at school. Some take refuge in the cliché that *boys will be boys*. Others wonder whether gender-segregated classrooms are the answer. Still others are open to multiple perspectives.

Not surprisingly, the *Newsweek* (Jan. 30, 2006) claim that "Girl behavior becomes the gold standard. Boys are treated like defective girls" has seized public attention and polarized the school gender learning debate. While headlines like the one in *Newsweek* cry *The Boy Crisis: At Every Level of Education, They're Falling Behind. What to Do?*, may perhaps stimulate useful public debate, I am concerned when it appears that rather than thoughtful, in-depth explorations of the complexities around gender learning inequities in schools, media reports and blogs offer eight-second sound bites and expedient solutions. I am also concerned when opportunities for exploration and debate become reduced to a single question: whether or not to segregate by gender.

Over the past few weeks several teachers and principals have emailed me about the growing single-gender schooling lobby in Ontario. What is being left out of the debate? For some the image of boys in ties, white shirts, and blazers arm-wrestling with a revered male teacher can have a nostalgic Mr. Chips kind of appeal. Others assume and imagine that boys and girls have such innate learning differences that east is east, and west is west, and never the twain should meet. It's all too easy to oversimplify the idea that boys are biologically programmed for kinesthetic visual-spatial activities and girls are programmed for collaboration and relational activities; that boys thrive with action and visual learning while girls respond best to relational reading and writing, rather than to recognize that these are general learning tendencies that express themselves differently across a broad continuum.

In my view, it is more productive to explore possible educational approaches that could benefit boys and girls—project-based and collaborative learning, multiple literacies, and differentiated classroom instruction, for example— than to latch onto a one-size-fits-all solution.

The Pressure for Achievement

Of course, in our rapidly changing and technologically complex society, when schools are under tremendous pressure to educate the most diverse student body in history to higher and higher academic standards, it can be tempting, when a simple-sounding remedy appears, to grab onto it and hold tight. It's not surprising that many parents whose boys are bored and disenchanted with school are attracted to the idea that single-gender classrooms could help make schools more hospitable to boys. Parents who are worried about their son's underachievement may resonate with claims that schools, where the majority of teachers are female, are over-feminized; that classroom instruction has been designed for girls, not boys; and the idea, which they have all along suspected and that is now confirmed by brain science, that boys and girls are two different species altogether.

While I appreciate that single-gender classrooms may be appropriate at times, I would ask that we resist the impulse for quick fixes and consider the wider view, the larger cultural context where gender inequities are interwoven with class, ethnicity, sexuality, and other factors. Before we weigh in on the potential benefits of single-gender classrooms, we would be prudent to first seek multi-layered understanding about boys' local realities and find solutions that launch from these realities.

Looking at Socio-Economic Factors

Having provided professional development for several staffs of prestigious boys' only private schools that offer outstanding educational opportunities, I am familiar with their local realities, especially the wealth of resources available to teachers and the boys. Imagine boys having choices from over three dozen extracurricular activities, including highly competitive sports, arts, technologies, and even philanthropic pursuits. I suspect that the academic success of these students is due less to gender segregation than to the abundant supports and resources available to them.

While there is no absolute consensus on the reality and scope of the education crisis for boys from the dominant ethno-cultural tradition, there's no doubt among researchers that our public schools are failing poor minority students in general and poor minority boys in particular. Poverty often contributes to a host of problems, including emotional disturbances, at home, in school, and in the wider community. And while we know that gifted minds are distributed equally across socio-economic classes, there is usually less support for gifted students who are economically disadvantaged.

I recall how, at a professional development day in an eastern Canadian community, educators struggled to make sense of painful and discouraging data: the staggering underachievement among boys who comprised one-hundred percent of early school leavers and one-hundred percent of those diagnosed with ADHD. As these caring teachers reflected on why boys comprised ninety percent of students who were not promoted to Grade 9 and were also recipients of ninety percent of school suspensions, they recognized that the relationship between gender and achievement is more multifaceted than they initially assumed. They acknowledge that while biological sex is assigned at birth, gender is something that we learn, and the nuances of what it means to be male vary from one community to another. As the teachers reflected on the diverse learning needs of their boys, they also speculated about the effects of poverty in their community. When the idea of single-gender classes came up, the suggestion was tabled. These thoughtful educators could see that before rushing to separate boys and girls, many other ideas needed to be explored.

Putting Brain Science about Gender in Perspective

Since the advent of brain image scanning tools, there has been much interest in the applications of brain science and gender to education. Many wonder if biological brain differences may partially explain the academic achievement gap between boys and girls.

Reports of research on gender differences in the brain in books such as *Brain Sex* show that boys' development, on average, lags about a year and a half behind girls' development. On average boys acquire speech clarity and the readiness to read at a later point than girls; girls typically take in more sensorial information, and are more attentive to their surroundings; the majority of boys arrive at kindergarten with fewer social skills such as turn-taking; girls, who are more likely to have increased levels of serotonin, have, on average, higher tolerance levels for frustration.

Often missing from the conclusions drawn from gendered brain science is the understanding that brain differences reveal relative tendencies, or averages.

Averages, which are statistical and mathematical means used to describe the general differences between populations, do not tell the complete story. For example, knowing that the average height of an adult male is 175 centimetres and female is 162 centimetres does not help us to predict a given individual's height. These numbers do not reveal that some women are taller than men. They do not explain individual differences. Imagine trying to assign a group of adolescents to two changerooms based solely on their heights: a tall students' changeroom and a short students' changeroom. This absurd scenario highlights the potential pitfalls of dividing students by gender: Learning about average statistical tendencies may lead us to exaggerate differences between boys and girls and thus limit our understanding of their needs. Knowing that the average boy finds it easier than a typical girl to construct buildings from two-dimensional blueprints does not explain why another boy has difficulty interpreting the same blueprint. In *Boy Smarts*, I say: "The binary gender construct, where the world is sharply divided between boys and girls, men and women, limits our understanding of people. Some boys are more aggressive and demanding like *Rambo* while others are more sensitive. In reality, gender exists along a continuum from extremely feminine at one end and extremely masculine at the other with many types of shading of gendered states in between."

When we reflect on the many varied ways that boys and girls learn, we may question such odd proclamations such as ones made by Leonard Sax, the spokesperson of the American single-sex movement in schools in a radio interview: "Boys do best in school when they are yelled at by female teachers" or "Any time you have a teacher of one sex teaching children of the opposite sex, there's a potential for a mismatch…If a male teacher speaks in a tone of voice that seems normal to him, a girl in the front row may feel that he is yelling at her." If we extrapolated from this inference, we might feel compelled to make sweeping changes to schooling, restricting male teachers to the teaching of boys, and female teachers to the teaching of girls. However, even in the boys' only schools where I have provided professional development, the majority of teachers were female. It is not the *gender* of the teacher that determines student success, it is the *quality* of teaching that has the most profound impact.

Alternatively, we might utilize the emerging field of brain science to recognize that although boys may have a preference toward visual-spatial learning, through the wonders of neuroplasticity—the ability of the brain to adapt and develop new neural pathways—all learners benefit from multiple approaches to learning, including physical and visual forms of engagement. The 2007 **Organisation for Economic Cooperation and Development** report that summarized the international data on brain development, *Understanding the Brain: The Birth of a Learning Science,* reveals that no study to date has shown gender-specific processes involved in building networks in the brain during learning.

Recognize the Culture of Masculinity in Schools

Differences between boys and girls' experiences in school go far beyond obvious biological differences.

Where teaching and learning were once thought as gender-neutral and free of bias, we have become uncomfortably aware of ways in which differences in the cultures of masculinity and femininity influence attitudes toward teaching and learning. Gender biases are expressed in the power structure of the school structure—in the ways that people work together and treat each other—all of which send important messages about gender expectations to both boys and girls. The versions of masculinity and femininity that are inculcated in classrooms become part of students' social identities. A boy's perception of his place in the world affects his motivation and his achievement.

The idea that masculinity represents a fixed, inevitable, and natural state of being is a myth. Each community defines what it deems to be masculine in its cultural context.

Across many cultures, however, males commonly shield their vulnerability. In North America, males are bombarded with unhealthy cultural messages from popular culture about what it means to be masculine. While boys' interpretations of these messages depend on their life circumstances and personal resiliency, among other things, many boys have concluded that doing well in school is not cool.

Might single-gender education create a different kind of culture where boys' achievement can be better supported?

The Jury Is Not In

Studies supporting single-gender education offer data suggesting that segregated learning environments enhance achievement. For example, the **Australian Council for Educational Research,** which released a longitudinal study of over 250,000 students in 2000 that shows how both boys and girls educated in single-gender classrooms scored on average fifteen to twenty-two percentile ranks higher on a range of achievement outcomes than boys and girls in co-educational settings.

However, studies supporting co-educational learning indicate any potential benefits of single-gender education were undermined because gender stereotypes are only reinforced in single-gender classrooms and in some cases stereotypical behaviours were worsened. A recent three-year California study concluded that small classes, strong curricula, dedicated teachers, and equitable teaching practices influenced the academic success of both girls and boys more than single-gender learning.

The 2009 international report on gender and achievement, *Equally Prepared for Life? How 15-year-old Boys and Girls Perform in School*—prepared by the **OECD**—revealed that in countries like Korea and Australia, where data indicated a significant difference in achievement for males in single-gender schools compared to those in co-ed schools, these differences disappeared after the schools socio-economic levels were taken into consideration.

It can be perplexing to parents and teachers alike when an educational institution makes wide and sweeping claims about the effectiveness of single-gender classes. The **Atlanta School District** website offers a *Single-gender Fact Sheet* indicating "the research is clear" and claims that in addition to improved academic achievement and graduation rates, the numbers of students attending college increases. They even boldly declare that "In 100 percent of studies on career aspirations of students, students in single-gender schools set higher goals to attain." While their data may reflect the reality in Atlanta, is their solution to under-achievement among youth as clear as this district professes for the rest of us? Why are many other experts flagging caution—and even alarm—about separating boys and girls for learning purposes?

It can be perplexing when a recently revised American federal law—the same law that protected racial inequality in earlier decades—despite their own acknowledgement that their research of single-gender learning is inconclusive, now allows US public schools to split up boys and girls. The American data overwhelming point to race and class as the strongest determinants of achievement. I believe we should be careful to avoid framing the discourse around gender and learning as a binary trap. As the **Australian Secondary Principals' Association** recently announced: "A gender apartheid approach would fail to recognize the complex nature of gender."

Consider Differentiated Instruction

I believe that we can help boys to be more themselves without segregating them from girls, without pitting their needs against the needs of girls, and without ignoring those who are economically or intellectually disadvantaged or who are marginalized in other ways.

One approach to accommodating diversity that many educators are turning to is differentiated instruction—the art and craft of building on students' individual learning needs.

This person-centered instruction means creating multiple paths of learning so that students of different abilities, interests, and personalities experience equally appropriate ways to absorb, use, develop and present their understandings and learning. Differentiated instruction encourages students to take greater responsibility and ownership for their own learning, and provides opportunities for peer teaching and cooperative learning.

Differentiated instruction steers clear of traditional stand and deliver methods of instruction and offers students multiple options for taking in information; options for making sense of ideas; and flexible options for students to express what they know. It understands that some students might create an annotated diagram of a scientific process or even create a podcast rather than write an essay about it. Visual learners might be invited to use graphic organizers, maps, diagrams or charts to integrate and reveal their comprehension of ideas. Students of differing levels of cognitive processing might produce graphic organizers or charts of differing levels of complexity.

Differentiated assessment also provides students with more than one way to demonstrate proficiency. While the goals of the assessment don't change, the formats, support systems, and time can vary with the goal of maximizing the opportunity for each student to show what he or she has learned. Differentiated instruction assumes that all students are capable, even though they may show their capabilities in different ways.

Differentiated instruction is one of many approaches to education that may help instill in our boys—indeed, in all students—a sense of community and global citizenship, healthy intellectual skepticism, respect for others, and appreciation for our abundant diversity.

Developing a Holistic Response to Meet the Needs of All Students

In *Boy Smarts,* I argue that we need to respond to address the learning needs of students in each school community in holistic ways that do not pit boys' educational needs against the needs of girls. While I am not, on principle, opposed to single-gender classrooms, I believe we should take our time to reflect and examine the subtle ways in which gender expectations and biases play out in our school communities and assess the needs of the students in our local communities.

Consider how your school community might respond to the following questions regarding gender and schooling:

- Are there significant differences between boys' and girls' achievement levels? If so, at which grade(s) do these differences manifest? Are there trends or trajectories that you notice?

- Are teachers responsive to varied needs for movement and spatial stimulation?

- Does your school staff manage girls' and boys' misbehaviour differently?

- Are children with high kinesthetic needs held in at recess or lunchtime? If so, what other options can you envision?

- Under what conditions are children suspended or sent home? Are there creative alternatives to suspensions that you have tried?

- Is there equal representation of boys and girls in behavioural and learning assistance programs?

- Is instructional attention distributed fairly, giving both boys and girls the chance to participate?

- Are opportunities and resources related to instruction, clubs, and athletics distributed equitably to boys and girls?

- Do school policies and practices ensure equality of opportunity for both boys and girls?

- Are there particular courses where it seems possible that gender separation could advance learning for both boys and girls? What are those circumstances, and what would be the rationale for this separation? Can you identify any potential pitfalls as well as potential advantages?

As you brainstorm around these questions, and as other questions crop up, you might consider developing a school-wide approach to raising boys' achievement. A conceptual framework that contains guiding principles should go beyond a focus on grades, and emphasize the development of strengths, gifts, and capacities.

With the support of others, you can find ways to help all students—especially those most vulnerable populations—thrive in the twenty-first century.

BOYS & SCHOOL SUCCESS

· · · · · · · · · ·

A Fable about Schooling: The Animal School

THE following fable beautifully illustrates the challenges I have seen fitting students, subjects, outcomes, time slots, grades, and personalities into school systems.

Once upon a time the animals decided they must do something heroic to meet the problems of a *new world* so they organized a school. They had adopted an activity curriculum consisting of running, climbing, swimming and flying.

To make it easier to administer the curriculum, all the animals took all the subjects.

The duck was excellent in swimming. In fact, better than his instructor. But he made only passing grades in flying and was very poor in running. Since he was slow in running, he had to stay after school and also drop swimming in order to practice running. This was kept up until his webbed feet were badly worn and he was only average in swimming. But average was acceptable in school so nobody worried about that, except the duck.

The rabbit started at the top of the class in running but had a nervous breakdown because of so much makeup work in swimming.

The squirrel was excellent in climbing until he developed frustration in the flying class where his teacher made him start from the ground up instead of the treetop down. He also developed a charlie-horse from over-exertion and then got a C in climbing and D in running.

The eagle was a problem child and was disciplined severely. In the climbing class, he beat all the others to the top of the tree but insisted on using his own way to get there.

At the end of the year, an abnormal eel that could swim exceeding well and also run, climb and fly a little had the highest average and was valedictorian.

The prairie dogs stayed out of school and fought the tax levy because the administration would not add digging and burrowing to the curriculum. They apprenticed their children to a badger and later joined the groundhogs and gophers to start a successful private school.

This story was written by George Reavis,
Assistant Superintendent of the Cincinnati Public Schools in 1940.

As parents we spend our family life affirming that each person is a unique individual, with differing outlooks and needs. In our schools teachers too are acutely aware that what motivates one student can be discouraging for another. We know that there is no one absolute way to teach all children, but there are many ways to teach each child one at a time.

The Animal School is a timeless fable that contains a powerful, universally understood message: Sweeping educational reforms that superficially respond the issues at hand don't work. Fuelled by optimism from the current leadership of the day, years of school reform have taught us that one-size-fits-all approaches will, undoubtedly, set our students up to fail.

While we appreciate that a boy's physiology marches on toward manhood, a boy's inner world needs to be drawn out—invited, coaxed, and challenged—toward authenticity and integrity. Over the years I have met many boys who are labelled as bad, to only find out that these boys are sad. Mostly I have discovered that boys are discouraged and distressed as they struggle to express their unmet needs. Our job is to look beyond their paltry achievement as well as their stormy behaviour and discover what is really going on. What is he trying to say?

26 Flexible & Creative Educators Help Turn Failure Into Success

HOW do we engage boys who have gotten off track and are on a collision course with failure?

How do we influence and lead these boys from a site of risk to a site of resilience?

In my visits to school communities to discuss how resiliency is encouraged, I have discovered the varied ways teachers, support staff, and administrators creatively respond to youth who buck the system. By adapting to their non-traditional styles of learning and guiding them to develop and tap into their own resourcefulness, passionate and caring adults can re-engage youth in schooling.

The following parental story highlights one boy's distinctive path to learning. Although he was derailed along his adolescent path, isolating himself from the support he so urgently needed, school staff initiated a turnaround experience for her son.

> **Dear Barry,**
>
> My son Aanand, a teenage slacker-in-the-making with activity levels that would leave most heads spinning, would tell me that school was not on his *radar*. With each passing year his spotty grades and attendance grew worse, until Grade 8 when he stopped trying all together and basically dropped out. I felt helpless to get him back on track. Sadly, so did the school.
>
> Whenever I'd meet with school staff they'd tell me they couldn't help him if he didn't want to *help himself*. I dearly wondered how my wayward son would help himself when he seemed more infatuated with impressing

peers with his latest skateboard *Airwalk* than achieving at school. [For those of you unfamiliar with skateboarding, a skater *Airwalks* when he makes an airborne walking motion with his legs after he grabs the nose of his skateboard as he negotiates himself off a ramp.] Frustrated with their lack of interest, ingenuity, and professionalism, mostly, I felt as though I had failed my son.

A shift in our malaise came to light during his final months of Grade 9, when some very caring and knowledgeable staff introduced a new approach. Dreading false hope, I was cautiously buoyed by their interest in his education and discussions about his strengths and talents, but I was mostly encouraged by the talk about how to make school fit Aanand's *skateboarder* outlook on life. Over the years I had come to believe that school was only for the kids who fit the proverbial square peg of schooling, but during the fall of Grade 10 it became clear that this staff was onto something good.

As I read your recent article about cultivating resiliency, I considered how Aanand was nudged toward success this past year in Grade 10. While the staff practised many of your suggestions, I believe that Aanand's recent success was mostly due to caring staff and their flexible learning designs. These teachers took the time to figure out his learning style and then helped Aanand to understand why his kinesthetic approach to learning had failed him in the past. Instead of hinting that he might need medical intervention—as numerous previous teachers had over the years—for his surplus activity levels they took it upon themselves to ramp up activity themselves and provided lively and appealing assignments. They spoke to him in a way that acknowledged his unique style of learning and Aanand finally began to listen. They clarified both what he needed to do as well as what they needed to do to spark and grow his learning. They took the time to notice that he was impossible in the morning and that his brain didn't seem to kick in until 11am, and ensured that his academic courses were in the later part of the school day. They worked with his personality and slowly connected with the real Aanand. They learned that my son thinks with his hands and has to be doing something physical to engage his brain. They even helped him to film a few of his skateboarder moves and upload them to **YouTube**. It wasn't until a couple of months later that I discovered the logic in their approach when he continued to complete many of his assignments through the movie clips he so carefully produced.

While caring connections with staff initially got his attention it was their flexibility that really held his interest in the long run. He became part of a unique school program along with twenty other Grade 10 students who spent the first half of their day—2 of 4 blocks—with a teacher, learning support teacher, and a youth worker and the remaining time in regular classes where he focussed on essential learning only: English 10 and Social Studies 10. It also made sense that the same teacher taught him both of these courses and was in regular communication with his learning support team. It was the kind of assistance that surrounded him with support so to speak, but did not restrict him. They gave Aanand room to be Aanand.

As you pointed out in your article, Aanand's growing resilience was more complicated than a *bounce back* from adversity. There was no single event that turned him around, but a series of daily encounters with learning that step-by-step taught him that he was capable and that he had smarts. He wasn't getting lost in the shuffle anymore. During his morning support blocks the teachers and youth worker took time to review his English and Social Studies assignments and gently challenged him to complete them while also giving him the real help that he needed. They recognized that Aanand often needed them to scribe for him while they engaged him in deeper discussion about assignments and how to make on-going alterations that tailored assignments to fit him. I doubt that he will ever become a keen writer, but I trust that he will learn to write for the times when he really needs to.

Aanand's newfound glimmer of hope grew over the year into more regular attendance and real achievement. The first couple of times he skipped or arrived to school smelling of *pot* I feared that he was doomed, but they took his behaviour in stride and never over-reacted. They did not corner him by laying down the law or threatening him with contracts or suspensions. Instead, they focussed on him as a person, his learning, and redirected him with dialogue about future goals. I'll not forget the day he announced to me during a late night pizza snack that he wanted to become a carpenter. I still get tears of gratitude and pride as I recall that moment when he explained that soon in Grade 11 he'd be in a co-op program where he would spend two weeks at school followed by two weeks in a carpentry-training apprentice. It was a perfect fit. As a younger boy he was drawn to building things with whatever he could get his hands on. It only made sense that he would do the same as an adult.

A key part of Aanand's success stemmed from the school staff accelerating him through Grades 8 and 9 and getting him into age-appropriate learning in Grade 10. I know they would have lost him if they tried to make him to complete English 8 when he was supposed to be in English 10. I wondered about how he'd make up for the gaps in his learning, but teachers assured me that this was the focus of their support in the morning.

You might also be interested to know that at home I noticed small changes over the year too, like Aanand keeping his room just slightly above toxic waste dump levels, and him appearing in the kitchen to eat with me on a more regular basis. Late one Saturday night I also overheard Aanand take the side of learning when he and his buddies returned home reeking of the concert mosh-pit's hallucinogenic haze. His buddies were discussing plans for skipping school Monday when my son muttered with no trace of self-consciousness that he couldn't skip that week and that his carpentry project was due.

With all this talk about cutbacks in education, I do fear that funding for apprenticeship programs will be eliminated. While I know that his learning success has grown in leaps and bounds over the past year, also I suspect that he is not out of the woods and he needs continued support. I hope that educational leaders and government officials holding the funding strings of power listen to success stories like my sons. School has made the difference between Aanand seeing himself as a *dropout* to a person with something genuinely good to offer. Thank you to the wonderful teachers who made learning work for Aanand.

27   The Curveball of Learning

FREQUENTLY, parents and teachers approach me after a presentation to offer heartwarming stories about their encounters with boys. Not only are their anecdotes informative, but they also illuminate how easily we can help or hinder boys' journeys to becoming caring, courageous and ethical men. I am pleased to share with you a gratifying story from Mike Ward, an experienced BC teacher about two boys in his class.

The Baseball Caper

Last week, two of the boys in my Grade 5 class gave me an unforgettable lesson in what it means to be an elementary-aged school boy.

When Connor arrived at school last Thursday, he was quick to seek out his friend, Wade, eager to show him his new baseball mitt. Connor, excited about trying it out and, since he didn't have a baseball, suggested that a nearby chunk of rock might admirably serve the purpose.

Wade, no stranger to trouble, hesitated for just a moment.

"Come on," urged Connor. "You pitch it and I'll be the catcher. I want to try out my mitt."

Shrugging off a fleeting apprehension, Wade picked up the rock. He paced off a suitable distance, turned, and fired.

It was a perfect pitch.

Connor barely had to time to blink.

The rock passed over the top of his glove, and struck him squarely between the eyes.

It sliced open his forehead and ricocheted off the underlying bone.

Even as Connor attempted in vain to stop the gushing blood from his wound with his hands, Wade ran to hide in the portable, knowing he would be blamed for Connor's misfortune.

As teachers collected, attempting to staunch the flow of blood, Connor was quick to point out it wasn't his friend's fault at all.

"I asked him to throw it, and I missed," he stated calmly and honestly.

After Connor's parents were alerted by the school administrators, Wade was located and brought out to the parking lot. He had just enough time to wish his friend well on his trip to the doctor.

Aftermath

Wade and Connor were very fortunate to have an understanding principal who raised four boys of his own.

This understanding principal concluded that:

1. The situation was not covered by the school prohibition against throwing rocks. This was clearly a sports related injury.

2. Connor deserved credit for admitting that he was doubly at fault for asking the rock to be thrown, and, for failing to catch it.

3. Wade was not to be held solely accountable. Who could have foreseen that a simple game of catch might result in so much bloodshed?

4. If blame was to be considered, surely Connor's parents played a role: what could have they been thinking to give a boy a mitt, but not a ball?

Wade's first reaction—tears—was a legitimate response to a stressful situation, exacerbated by an innately male inability to vocalize fear and concern. Wade, in fact, deserved some credit too for calming himself in time to wish his friend well at the hospital.

Epilogue

Connor has learned an important sports lesson—always keep your eye on the ball—and Wade has discovered a hitherto overlooked ability to deliver a projectile within the strike zone.

Importantly, the boys remained good friends.

In fact, Wade has promised to show Connor his new water propelled rocket launcher this weekend.

What harm could there be in that?

This wise teacher and principal understood that children can learn from their missteps and recover from failure, and eventually learn to treat others with respect—as much respect as we provide them.

28   Responding Creatively to Masked Anxiety

IT'S common for boys to try to draw adults into an argument to scuttle a discipline discussion—especially when they are troubled or anxious. Teachers and parents may become triggered and find themselves reacting instead of responding. During these times it's important to remember that it is the certainty of the response—not the severity or intensity—that makes the impact. It is adult responsiveness and calm follow-through that speaks of commitment and care. Sometimes we can think that boys learn more from a stronger consequence such as being publicly shamed, sent to the office, or suspended, but the results of these tactics usually include alienation and resentment.

Below, you will find my response to a school administrator's inquiry about dealing with a boy's hallway bravado, and suggestions for helping a boy resolve conflict while addressing issues that may underlie a show of toughness.

Transformative Teacher Listens Beyond Bravado

Hello Barry,

As a vice-principal in a large secondary school, I am often called to intervene when students violate our school's code of conduct. Recently, a parent challenged one of our teacher's disciplinary response to her son, who name-called this teacher in the hallway. The parent suggested that the teacher had backed her son into a corner with his authoritarian approach, heightening conflict between them. She claimed that her son had a lot of anxiety and that the teacher had not provided him with enough time to cool down.

The parent requested that we read your book, *Boy Smarts,* and in particular one of your guidelines: ***Listen Beyond Bravado***. We did and it makes sense, but now I'd appreciate if you could provide our staff with a specific example of how a conversation might unfold between a troubled student and a teacher so we can put this guideline into action. The more specific you could be the better. Thanks.

Tom

Hello Tom,

Recently, a secondary teacher at a school workshop relayed to me a hallway conflict that he encountered with a Grade 9 boy that sounds similar to the incident at your school. Your staff might find it interesting to consider this teacher's story as they strengthen their own understanding of boys who present as anxious, angry, and resistant. Consider the following scenario of a typical power struggle between teacher and student:

On the way to my classroom after a busy Friday lunch, I overhead a boy named Brad, from my Grade 9 math class. He was *dissing* me, telling his friends that I was an *idiot*. I stopped dead. As I looked straight into his eyes, the hustle of the hallway was instantly muted. Rolling his eyes in disgust, Brad turned his back, muttering audibly, "Any teacher who gives that much homework is an idiot." You could hear a pin drop as he began rifling through his locker.

In that instant it seemed that everyone in the hallway was watching me, waiting for me to do something. Several students, another teacher, and the vice-principal had stopped to watch the drama.

Out of the corner of my eye I felt the vice principal's eyes on me. I sensed that he wanted me to discipline this boy, to set an example of him.

I also felt Brad's friends grinning, cheering him on silently, hoping for a showdown.

I cleared my throat. It was time to speak, to show who was in charge. I could issue an edict: send Brad to the office, tell him in no uncertain terms that he couldn't use that kind of language.

Yet I had been struggling to form a connection with Brad, and I knew that this reactivity would cost me in the classroom.

What should I do in such a moment?

At times some boys may know that they are transgressing, and that they will get caught eventually, but they want to appear as if they are in control. When boys spout off, we can also consider whether they are only attempting to manage their anxiety and frustration in unskilled ways.

When a boy's heels are dug in, adults need to pull back to avoid escalating the situation. If we insist that students do things our way, we risk raising the stakes in a new, heightened level of confrontation. What do students learn when we get ensnared in counterproductive arguments or aggravating power struggles? Insisting on doing things his own way can be the boy's method of showing he is his own boss, which can be productive for him on one level. It can also be a way of avoiding his anxiety. Eye-rolling, muttering, and smiling at inopportune moments are meant to provoke us and also to save face. When a boy like Brad throws the teacher a rope to tussle over, the teacher must be conscious enough not to grab the rope.

Consider how Brad has orchestrated this confrontation, consciously or not, by choosing the stage(the hallway near his locker), the audience (his friends), the issue (quantity of homework), and finally the time (a hectic and stressful time of day and week). A teacher who grabs this rope is sunk. Rather than engaging in a tug of war with Brad, the teacher can take the opportunity to engage with Brad about his deeper concerns—homework and achievement.

Avoid Immediate Hallway Response

Repeatedly, I see adults who, while trying to impose discipline, lose their connections to boys when they are drawn into games of status. The result is that boys quickly dig in, and revert to tough talk in the attempt to save face.

The best response is to say to Brad, firmly but kindly: "I need to speak with you after class this afternoon." Do not wait for his answer. Turn and walk away. Do not respond to anything he or his friends might mutter at this point. *Understand that it's the certainty of your response and not the severity.*

Conversational Considerations

Before talking with Brad, give yourself enough time and space to make sure you are calm yourself. Begin with a neutral, matter-of-fact consideration of what happened—the event. Be careful to avoid triggering defensiveness by describing behaviour with negatively charged, accusatory words. "Why were you so rude?" will not invite cooperation, and will only get Brad's back up.

As you talk, recognize that fidgeting and avoiding eye contact are frequently other ways that boys speak with their body to let you know that they are feeling anxious and may need help to process the discussion. Avoid insisting that Brad stand, sit still, or look at you, and you most likely will observe that the fidgeting helps him to relax as you maintain connection while getting information.

Be aware that even though a boy's language is sometimes harsher than we like, we need to listen for what's underneath. It is often wiser to simply wait quietly rather than saying something right away. If we are to tap into a boy's motivation for learning and social connection, we must listen for underlying needs. Active listening communicates empathy and caring, while opening up opportunities for problem solving and insight.

Sample Dialogue Between Teacher and Student After Class

Teacher: "Thanks for coming in (sits in a neutral chair and not behind teacher desk). I know it's been a long week—it has been for me too—and I appreciate your time."

Student: "Whatever" (looks away).

Teacher: "I'd like to talk with you about what happened between the two of us in the hallway earlier today. I'm thinking there's a problem brewing and I want to know how we can work things out" (teacher looking out the window and not directly at the student).

Student: "Yeah, sure" (eyes roll).

Teacher: "You seemed angry with me in the hallway earlier" (mirrors Brad's minimal eye contact).

Student: "I wasn't talking to you (face begins to flush). I was talking to my friends. Is there a law about talking to friends about a teacher in the hallway?"

Teacher: "You're frustrated with me."

Student: "Yeah" (body stiffens and he looks away). "Your stupid homework!"

Teacher: "You're angry about the amount of math homework I assigned."

Student: "Yeah. It sucks. How do you expect anybody to do it?"

Teacher: "You don't like the assignment."

Student: "Yea. That's what I said, didn't I?"

Teacher: "This helps me to understand what's going on. You were keeping up with most of the assignments until this unit" (pause). "Tell me more about what you think about this math we're doing."

Student: "That other stuff was easier. I just don't get what you are trying to teach us."

Teacher: "This new math unit is tough" (pause). I'm guessing that you're discouraged about not getting it because you like to keep on top of things" (pause). "This homework only makes things worse—adds insult to injury, so to speak."

Student: "Yeah! Can I go now?"

Teacher: "We're almost done. I just need to know if there is anything else that's bothering you."

Student: "You make me feel like such a retard when you come over and try to help me in class. If you are such a math wiz, your scorebook will tell you that I'm failing. If you'd teach it more properly, more of us would understand what you are trying to teach."

Teacher: "Sounds as if you're really frustrated by not being able to understand this math" (pause). You also don't like it when I approach you in class to help you. You're uncomfortable about being singled out. By trying to help you in class I am actually making things worse for you."

Student: "Yeah. Just leave me alone. Are we done here?"

Teacher: "You might feel like you're the only one struggling so much with this unit, but I know others are having a hard time too. Can you come to my class after school so that I can see exactly where you need some coaching?"

Student: "I have plans after school."

Teacher: "What about during Monday's tutorial?"

Student: "We'll see."

Teacher: "That'd be great. I'll take a look at your last test this weekend and see if I can figure out where you started to get lost" (Brad nods, somewhat reluctantly). "Sounds like we've got a plan" (pause). "I still need to talk about where we got off track in the hallway earlier today. What happened?"

Student: "I was frustrated. Your math made me mad. I guess I just lost my cool."

Teacher: "Thanks for letting me know. Losing our cool is easy to do when we get frustrated."

Student: "Okay" (a look of relief comes over Brad's face).

Teacher: "See you Monday at tutorial. We'll figure it out."

Student: "See ya" (Turns and walks out of room).

Constructive Outcomes

During this brief encounter, the teacher managed to turn a potentially volatile incident into a chance for greater connection. He took charge of his own angry reaction to Brad's hallway insult by choosing to discuss the incident later, after they both had an opportunity to cool down. The teacher focussed on Brad's behaviour—not his character—by describing events and not evaluating them. By not demanding an apology from Brad and recognizing that in his own way Brad was acknowledging his part when he said: "I was frustrated...I guess I lost my cool," the teacher allowed Brad to save face, permitting him to maintain his sense of dignity. The teacher took responsibility for his contribution to the conflict: Brad's anxiety about not getting it in class was heightened when the teacher would try to help Brad in front of others. Finally, the teacher modelled respectful communication throughout the encounter by overlooking Brad's lack of cooperation and focussing on a strategy to move forward positively.

When a boy starts to talk about an incident, use simple prompts to encourage his story to unfold. Encouragements such as "I really want to hear what happened from your point of view," or "It's important for me to understand what caused you stress," keeps you outside of his conflict while drawing him out. If the retelling triggers more emotions, allow them to wash through. Modelling calmness yourself is important. Only when his arousal level is calmed, and he is willing to converse, can you start to explore what happened and begin to problem-solve.

29   Cultivating Capability

KNOWING we are capable is the true source of self-esteem.

It is easy for media headlines to bash caregivers for being too attentive, too focussed, and too protective of children. Both parents and teachers walk a fine line between doing for our children and encouraging and teaching them to do for themselves. Capability comes from learning that we can handle what life asks of us. There is no substitute for getting lots of practice in handling things as children, with the loving guidance of parents and caregivers.

How do we walk the line between helping our children and encouraging them to do for themselves?

Hello Barry,

A parent stormed into my office the other day protesting about the grade I gave her son. When I tried to address the underlying issue, she said I was unfair and left in anger. Her son has the academic ability to earn top marks in English, but he is not handing in top assignments and he is also not submitting them on time—they are often two or three weeks late. I know that my expectations are reasonable, but worry that this parent may just be too protective of her son, enabling him to underachieve. As a parent myself, I know that it's perfectly healthy to advocate for and protect your child. But how far is too far?

Curiously, over my twenty years of teaching, I have observed increasing attention to raising kids' self-esteem while indulging their whims. Just

Dear Marti,

Since the earliest of times parents, mentors, and teachers have helped children to develop independence and autonomy by scaffolding or supporting children's learning in appropriate ways, and gradually withdrawing their support as children develop increasing self-sufficiency.

Students benefit when parents take interest in their schooling and assignments, of course, while parents are also mindful not to break one of the cardinal rules of parenting: *Never do for a child that which he can do for himself.*

Recently, a father relayed his son's response to losing his new favourite toy at the community swimming pool: "That's okay, daddy. You can buy me another one." When the father indicated that he did not have the money to replace the toy, his son replied with a single word: "Visa."

Parents may be tempted to replace broken or lost toys immediately, but what does this quick gratification teach children?

Replacing broken and lost toys can do more harm than good. It can rob children of the opportunity to learn how to manage loss and disappointment. If we try to smooth out every disappointment, we may also rob our children of gratitude. When we interfere with developmentally appropriate childhood difficulties, it's a little like carrying a one year old around all the time: He doesn't learn to trust his own capacity for propelling himself forward, by crawling or walking himself.

At times parents naturally may wish to shield their children from excessive disappointment, fearing perhaps that loss or failure may cause their children to give up altogether. Although it can be difficult for some parents to keep a distance while their children flounder, excessive shielding robs children of the opportunity to develop insight and learn from their mistakes.

We know cognitively that we get stronger from facing disappointment and negotiating challenges, that true self-esteem comes, in part, from learning that we can engage in struggle. Children who test their competencies in safe and caring atmospheres, without fear of humiliation, learn to believe in themselves and in their ability to solve problems. They develop courage to face failure, to pick themselves up when they are down, to take risks and try out new possibilities. Even though we may long to rescue our children when we see them suffer, we know that we learn resilience from dealing with life's adversities. Indeed, when we observe from a distance and intervene only when absolutely necessary, children learn that we have faith in their ability to manage frustration as they work through life's hurdles.

We ache for our children to be successful at school and life. We long to keep them safe and secure. Ultimately, however, children need to learn how to speak their mind and advocate for themselves. The result of doing too much for our children is that they develop the false belief that they can get what they want, when they want it, and that these desires—often whims—will be met from outside themselves. They may also come to believe that there is something seriously wrong with the universe if their desires are not quickly satisfied. What's worse is that they may come to believe that they cannot work toward difficult goals.

Standing by While Kids Make Mistakes Takes Faith, Love, and Courage

Parents are often overwhelmed by pressures and worries their own parents never experienced. The demands on parents to keep up in this rapidly proliferating digital culture—marked by convenience, expedience, and instant gratification—are astounding. We worry that our children may post photos of themselves, drunk and half-naked, on *Facebook* for future employers to view. We wonder whether our children's *Wii-ing* and *IM'ing* might get them into trouble that we can't even contemplate. Exhausted by the perceived need to keep up ourselves in a variety of ways—measuring ourselves at times by the index of our children's apparent happiness and success—it can seem easier to just grab hold and do it ourselves.

In the age of *Facebook* and ubiquitous mobile phones, parents can be more involved in their children's lives than ever before. Micro-managing, micro-scheduling, and micro-enriching all aspects of our kids' lives can create a generation of children who require continual direction, continual bolstering, and continual micro-managing in return.

As a result, it becomes common for some kids to avoid tackling challenging tasks because they fear discomfort and distress.

Some of the best-intentioned parents and teachers may be tempted to give children's wants and demands priority over the collective good and common sense. When we focus too much on helping children feel good, we may think we are supporting them when we are inadvertently disabling them.

Being too helpful—hovering over them to ensure that they do not fail—actually makes youth feel helpless and incompetent. It may also give them power and authority, at home and at school, that they are not ready to handle.

I believe we can help children the most by fostering independence. Indeed, many of us would rather have a young adult son who could care for himself, whether or not he had advanced education, rather than a son who goes to university but is unable to fend for himself.

Teachers and parents who hover over children with too much solicitude may actually be teaching children to sit back, wait to be served, or even wait to be bailed out. These kids are at risk for later developing resentment when special service and rescue does not arrive. They can have a difficult time adjusting to life's challenges.

A Healthy Balance

Parents who wish to strike a healthy balance with school involvement would be wise to respect the needs of their maturing children who will need increasing opportunities to make decisions on their own—with guidance from caring adults at times.

There is no clear line about how much involvement is too much, as it depends on the needs of the child and the circumstance. Children who are very shy or have legitimate learning difficulties might need a parent to be more involved. However, we need to be discreet and sensitive about our interventions so that we do not take over, and smother these children's efforts, however tentative they are.

Bubble Wrapping Emotions

One of the positive ways we can support our children is to allow them to struggle and express emotions about stumbling blocks. When a boy returns from school complaining about his teacher or an assignment, don't rush to rescue him from frustration. Instead reflect and affirm his feelings with a brief statement such as "Tough day," or "You seem really angry about that." If he is old enough and receptive enough, you could ask a clarifying question about ideas he might have for possibly solving his problem. Unless he asks you specifically for advice, avoid telling him what you think he ought to do. Even then, rather than dispensing advice, it can often be helpful to express faith in his ability to figure it out, or asking him what he thinks could help in this situation.

If his anger is directed toward you, remember that anger is a powerful emotion that can sometimes be used to manipulate us to give in to demands. The only way out of a power struggle is to remain calm and refuse to argue. Even if your son says "I hate you," remember that not only is he simply expressing his rage of the moment; he may be saying "I hate it when I don't get my way." Respond calmly with a mirroring comment such as "I can tell you're really angry." In time he will learn that you can maintain your connection to him, even when he is agitated, but that you won't be manipulated by angry or unkind words. When faced with a calm parent who refuses to engage in a power struggle, your son is more likely to stop blaming outside forces, and look within.

When we recognize that our children can't always be happy, we are liberated to listen compassionately, maintaining our connectedness while our children struggle with their disappointments. We learn to appreciate that our children's unhappiness does not reflect our success and worth as parents.

Encouraging Independence: For Parents and Teachers

If you are a parent and want to avoid hovering while promoting age-appropriate independence, recognize that if your boy asks to do something by himself, it probably means that he is ready.

If you know he is capable of undertaking a task, but he is not yet asking to do for himself, you could suggest that he give it a try.

If you know that he is capable, but has developed a habit of relying on you, check that you are not enabling him by, for example, waking your son up in the morning; laying out his clothes and doing his laundry; making and packing his lunches; reminding him repeatedly to complete tasks; doing his chores for him; replacing his lost or broken items; and buying too many gifts for him.

If you have been providing these services for some time, don't go cold turkey tomorrow. Just as it would be unwise to teach someone how to swim by throwing them in the water, you can teach your son to take on new responsibilities by encouraging him to assume more and more age-appropriate responsibilities.

Teachers who encounter students who expect undue attention and special treatment can also foster independence by choosing not to cater to students. Be firm and kind. Ensure that you are assigning reasonable tasks and due dates, providing engaging learning opportunities, and teaching with passion.

Attuning to the student—helping him move to the next thing he is ready to learn—is your job, but completing assignments, meeting deadlines, and learning is the student's job.

As Linda Albert points out in *Cooperative Discipline*, and Betty Lou Bettner and Amy Lew also highlight in *Raising Kids Who Can,* self-esteem and faith in oneself comes not from having things made easy, but from the lived experience of feeling capable, connected to others, and knowing that you have something to offer.

Imagining at times that we are bolstering our children by reducing stress in their lives, we teach dependence on others for happiness, but when we pass over responsibilities to our children in developmentally appropriate ways, we foster independence and self-respect.

30 Developing Independence

IT is only natural that parents want to raise boys who can manage on their own later as adults while they also become a part of something bigger—a family, a community. Years ago on the family farm, children pitched in and helped with everyday chores, for instance gathering the eggs and tending to farm animals. Contributing by putting food on the table taught valuable lifelong skills.

Today, many parents are challenged to create a structure for children to make contributions in everyday natural ways.

How will boys learn to be successful when we do so much for them?

Hello Barry,

Your assertion that capability is connected to self-esteem is right on the button. It seems common-sensical, yet I find myself doing way too much for my boys. I feel so guilty about not having the time to teach them, let alone supervise them! It's less nerve-racking for my husband or I to clean and attend to laundry than get them to pitch in. It's also easier for the weekly cleaning service to disinfect the bathroom, vacuum their bedrooms, and change their bed sheets. Furthermore, my oldest claims that he has a demanding hockey schedule and I don't want to mess with his motivation, knowing that his enthusiasm for Grade 9 has petered out.

At times I do wonder how my underachieving Grade 6 son is going to make it in this world when he can't seem to find his running shoes or his schoolwork, or even brush his teeth without me haranguing him. I also lose sleep over the twins in Grade 1 as they coast along merrily without a worry while we all attend to their needs, including wiping noses when they drip.

I yearn for simpler times, recalling that my childhood antics came to a standstill until my room was cleaned; that the television was off-limits until the dishes were done; and that work always came before play.

Thankfully my husband and I equally share household responsibilities and flexibility in response to our demanding careers. As I wrestle with engaging our boys more, it would be helpful to know your thoughts about reasonable expectations and guidelines for boys to help with chores so that they learn to become independent. I especially want them to learn the value of contributing.

Augustina

Dear Augustina,

Many parents, like you, worry how children will learn the necessary skills they need to manage their own lives, livelihoods, and perhaps their own families in the future. No doubt our own parents had similar anxieties about us, even though we may remember our own youth as a kind of golden era.

Of course, our own harried lives—where convenience, expedience, and instant gratification rule—are very unlike our parents' lives. Those who study family life are concerned about how increasing demands on our time might be eroding opportunities for parents to teach life skills and deepen connections with their children. A recent study about the changing tempos of family life found that our workloads have increased to a 9.25 hour workday, seven days a week, with employed mothers averaging 10 hour workdays. With accelerated time pressures, we have less time to teach kids about household chores, and perhaps less time than our parents once did to model and teach practical skills such as cooking and cleaning. Indeed, few of us have been able to maintain the orderly and disciplined homes many of us once experienced.

Not surprisingly, while each generation of parents faces challenges unique to their time, children's basic needs remain unchanged. Children need not only love and care, but also increasing opportunities to develop self-esteem through increasing independence and responsibility. Learning to self-govern is a slow, graduated process. When 2 year old Johnny spills his juice, we gently guide him to wipe up. When Johnny is 4, we enlist his help to load the dishwasher. When he is 6, we may expect him to tear up lettuce for the salad or help a younger sibling get dressed. When he is 10, we expect him to rake the front yard leaves without any help or supervision.

But what if we don't take the time to teach our children to contribute in their earliest years? What if they don't learn to pick up those drooled *Captain Crunch* bits under chairs? What if they are not expected to pitch in and participate in household chores? What happens ten years down the road when adolescents decide it is not their job to walk the dog, load the dishwasher, or help prepare meals? What happens when older children prefer going out with their peers instead of taking care of household responsibilities? Will we give up, hoping that they'll figure out how to be responsible eventually?

Recent studies have found that today's children spend more time in childcare and organized activities and less time on household responsibilities than they did twenty years ago. Where kids in middle childhood once spent just under 5.5 hours a week contributing to household chores such as meal preparation, pet care, and yardwork, they now spend only three hours. Some parents may even be hard-pressed to tally an average of three weekly hours of chores for their kids.

As it turns out, doing household chores is also a major predictor of whether children will later contribute volunteer time or community work when they become adults. A recent study by Alice Rossi at the **University of Massachusetts Amherst** analysed information on more than 3,000 adults and found a strong link between learning to contribute as a child and making contributions as an adult.

While I am hesitant to oversimplify with my own granny's kitchen wisdom— "you don't work, you don't eat"—studies like this one can remind us that changing cultural conditions do not necessarily change our children's core needs for growing autonomy and the value of learning to contribute. Learning to share domestic chores has become a critical marriage-preservation skill for young men. Furthermore, providing service to others is often an indicator of mental health. It is my hope that the following guidelines will assist you to explore ways that your family will be strengthened as your boys pitch in more.

Recognize the Primacy of a Secure Attachment

Studies indicate that infants who are secure in their attachment to us are more likely to assume age-appropriate independence and responsibility during their teen and adult years. Infant research has shown that it is caregivers' sensitive responsiveness that teaches our very young that the world is a safe place and that we can be trusted. It is from this emotionally secure place children will later venture to experiment with their curiosity and explore their initiative, knowing that they can return for love and guidance when they feel uncertain or threatened.

Start Young

When boys are approaching their second birthday, build on their desire to try to be like us by encouraging their helpful behaviour in everyday chores. As you take time to do simple tasks together—taking out the garbage, putting toys away, or transferring clothing to the dryer—these contributions will become essential parts of their daily lives. Incorporate a clean-up routine into your playtime together. Consider inviting your son's help with putting groceries onto a checkout counter and handing you things to be put away into the kitchen pantry. By ages two or three, boys can also help make their beds by handing you their pillow or opening up the pillow case as you change sheets. Your knowledge about your son's personality and frustration level will help you to discern *doable* tasks from ones beyond his capability at a given stage of development.

Create Routines

Visit a primary classroom where children are happily learning and you'll discover an organized teacher who provides predictable routines for a reason: routines provide security for children as they experiment with independence.

When your son starts kindergarten, you might provide him with an alarm clock to wake him each morning for school. Asking him to take charge of how he starts his day sends a powerful message that you believe in him and that you expect him to grow and develop.

As you focus on routine responsibilities, your 4 or 5 year old son will likely be able to empty his bedroom garbage can; put dirty clothes in hamper; get the newspaper; push chairs in after meals, place napkins on the table and help clear the table and floor after meals.

Use routines to reinforce good habits. Encourage him to help with loading and unloading non-breakable items from dishwasher, sort laundry and transfer clothes from dryer to basket, and put toys away in particular spots.

Of course, boys will mess up and slack off at times, particularly when they are learning a new routine, but once a structured routine becomes familiar, they will be likely to cooperate. If your 12 year old son is having an off day, rather than getting frustrated with him, just say calmly, "You always feed the fish right before we set the table."

Lead By Example

Children eagerly learn through imitation and are often more influenced by what we do than by what we say. When we overhear our 4 year old child scolding a younger sibling with the same sharp tone that we recently used, we realize how unintentional role modelling and unplanned influences can be just as powerful as those we carefully design. Children copy our behaviour, whether we want them to or not.

Recently, a parent emailed claiming that in a moment of frustration she found herself lecturing: "What part of 'Don't touch that!' do you not understand?"

The following day her 6 year old son kept talking on about how tired he was, but she persisted with her prompts: "Come on—let's get going!" She was humbled when he retorted: "What part of 'I'm tired' did you not understand?"

The same holds true for older boys who absorb values around the ways we prioritize and distribute our time between work and family life. They learn from us when we make decisions to stick to our budget rather than overextend our financial limits in a moment of weakness. While you need to respect that your oldest boy has a demanding hockey schedule, you would be wise to still insist that he contribute to the family's well-being with chores you both agree on. He might, for example, cook a meal one night per week, vacuum the entire house on the weekends, and regularly cut the lawn in the summer.

Take Time to Explain

Explaining what we are doing and why we are doing it can further our children's learning. It's easy to forget how kids can be mystified by chores we have routinely been doing for ages. Whether we are completing a chore or contributing outside of the home, our children are more likely to understand our motivation and behaviour when we explain what we are doing, and why.

When beginning to clean a messy room, you might share your thought processes out loud, saying: "Oh, this place is such a mess, I don't know where to begin." It is likely that you'll be mirroring your son's own thoughts about his bedroom. Showing how you begin a task—"I guess I'll just dive into this closet and see how far I get before lunch"—demonstrates how to manage overwhelming tasks and highlights the value of breaking them down into manageable chunks.

Getting older boys involved in more complicated household chores—price comparison shopping, caring for the car, cleaning counters and floors, managing laundry—will prepare teens for becoming self-sufficient later.

Hold Family Meetings

While many families have meetings only when crises occur, consider having weekly family meetings—perhaps while walking through a local park or sitting around the dinner table. These meetings give children opportunities for input on family life and teach how to operate by democratic dialogue or consensus rather than blind assumption. As you discuss varied topics such as planning the next family weekend road trip, making a schedule for chores, or purchasing a family computer, children will garner skills in problem solving and collaborative decision-making—skills highly valued in today's world.

Experiment with meeting formats that best suit family needs. When our boys were younger, they enjoyed a clearly organized meeting structure and the chance to experiment with official roles as chairperson or recorder, but as they got older, these formalities detracted from problem solving practice, so we relaxed the meeting format to reflect our evolving needs.

Focus On Effort

Remember that it's more important to notice and comment on your son's effort and desire to contribute, rather than on whether chores are completed perfectly. When you notice your younger son overfilling the dog's water dish and spilling water onto the floor say: "I see that you are being very careful to get as much water in the bowl that you can. I hope Toby appreciates how much you care about him." Support him when he experiences frustration or difficulty by helping him wipe up the spilled water, and you will further teach him the value of working with others to achieve success.

Pass Up the Temptation to Redo a Chore

Realize that your son will probably not complete the chore as efficiently or competently as you could at the beginning. It can be tempting to grab your son's clothes and fold them properly yourself. If you know he can do better, make a comment that uses your voice tone to convey your concern: "I guess that's an *okay* job with folding your T-shirts…". Your tone will be more than enough to get your point across.

Keep It Fun

Most people are more likely to enjoy tasks when they're lively and shared. You probably remember the saying: "Many hands make work light." Your 9 year old son will love helping to wash the car on a hot day if spraying you with the hose is part of the plan. Whatever the age, cleaning can easily become a game. Consider playing some music and swivel your hips as you vacuum the hallway or scrub that toilet.

Provide Choices

For toddlers, opportunities to contribute need to be simple and clearly defined. You could ask very young children to choose between taking the newspaper to the table or the oven mitts to the counter. They might choose colours for their bath towel or T-shirt. As boys get older, gradually offer them more freedom to make choices that affect them, within age-appropriate limits set by you.

Let Your Child Experience Consequences of His Choices

As long as the outcome isn't harsh or dangerous, let your son live with the results of his behaviour and his decisions. When he becomes distracted with a program on television and burns his toast, stay quiet and let the burnt toast be his teacher. Over time he will learn that actions lead to certain outcomes, both positive and negative. When we remain supportive, careful not to criticize poor choices, boys will more likely accept the consequences for their actions. Consider that when your older sons leave sports equipment outside in the rain overnight—a favourite skateboard perhaps—the wheel bearings may become rusty. Avoid interrupting his learning experience with an *I told you so* reminder that often only shifts his disappointment about the results of his negligence to resentment about your reminder.

If he's usually responsible for packing his lunch each morning and one day forgets, don't hand-deliver it to his classroom later. He may regret having forgotten his lunch, but you can bet he'll remember it the next day.

Sidestep Scolding

It can be tough to maintain your cool when your son repeatedly fails to comply with reasonable expectations. But lectures and punishments rarely work, at least not over the long haul, and they won't teach him self-discipline. Be firm, yet respectful, simply stating the chore agreement: "At the last family meeting we agreed that you would empty the dishwasher and your brother would load the dishwasher."

Another way to respond is through the use of humour, which wakes up the brain. Younger children especially love it when we behave in silly ways. Instead of reprimanding your youngster for leaving his breakfast bowl on the floor where the dog will undoubtedly find it, address the subject a little later by saying: "Let's pretend this is an empty bowl from breakfast. What can we do with it? We can (pause) wear it like a hat! Wouldn't that be silly? I know, we can (pause) turn it upside down and pretend it's a chair! Hey I know, we can (pause) put it in the sink!" While you both enjoy the foolishness of this game, your son will learn to compare solutions and will more likely place his cereal bowl in the sink the next morning.

Give Cues But Avoid Nagging

Many parents and teachers get exasperated with what they see as the need to repeat instructions day in and out, often several times a day: "How often do I have to tell you to hang up your wet jacket when you come inside?" Scolding reminders are unlikely to change behaviour, and are more likely to fuel negativity in your relationship. Sometimes, it can be more effective to use a nonverbal gesture by pointing to the desired solution. You might also refocus your instruction so the stimulus of coming in the door becomes the cue: "Go back outside, come back in, and hang your wet jacket where it can dry." Whether your cues are verbal or non-verbal, realize how a facial expression or tone of your voice can escalate conflict or help with constructive learning.

Caution: Cash for Chores

While money can be an incentive for boys who need a motivational boost, remember that helping out at home is part of being a member of your family. For this reason it is best to avoid tying allowance to everyday chores and paying children for being family members. While it may be reasonable to pay your son for something that you would typically pay someone else to do, such as washing your car, remember that hiring out your domestic chores may set up another predicament; for example, your boys may learn to buy into a gender stereotype in which the person who scrubs the toilet is a low-wage earning woman. For this reason many parents who work full time and can afford to hire help often choose not to.

Parents Aren't Perfect

These days most families live overscheduled and overwhelmed lives with precious few minutes remaining in the day to tackle chores. If your family is trapped in a time crunch, it may be time to reevaluate your priorities around work-life balance. You all benefit when everyone pitches in to help make your home a safe, ordered refuge from outside chaos and pressures.

Teaching children to contribute may be seen as teaching stewardship. By helping with chores, children internalize the realization that they are part of a larger whole, and that they have something meaningful to offer. As you consider your own boy's motivation to contribute, take into consideration your own track record. If you have consistently cleaned up after them over the years, they will likely become resistant if you expect too much too soon. Go slow and steady, but resist the urge to give in.

Finally, let's just accept that none of us are capable of perfect parenting or anything close to it. We don't always do what we say and say what we mean. We are human—as are our children—and we need the courage to be gentle with ourselves and our own limitations. As you manage the ups and downs of implementing household chores, avoid focussing on mistakes—whether yours or your son's. If we are to mentor boys to develop independence and a sense of self-worth in the family and the wider community, we need balance, perspective, and compassion toward ourselves and others. As you and your son rake up leaves or clean up after a meal, allow yourself a moment to breathe deeply, celebrating the small successes of everyday family life.

31   Fostering Resiliency

WHEN boys are trusted, given responsibility, and treated with respect, they move from a site of risk to a site of resilience. Compassionate, caring relationships, rigorous but realistic expectations, and opportunities for active participation help to engage all students in learning.

When boys seem discouraged and apathetic, can we activate their innate resilience?

Hello Barry,

My son's roller coaster ride through the elementary school years crashed in Grade 6. With the exception of Grades 2 and 4, and a few positive learning experiences here and there, written assignments have been especially tough for Michael. When he bottomed out last year, I met with our much-liked principal to discuss help for Michael next year in Grade 7. During our meeting he claimed that it was people *chemistry* that made the difference for Michael and that when his often-challenging behaviours clashed with his teacher's expectations, Michael dug in and turned away from learning. I am worried that Michael's education is at risk, that his final elementary school year will be a bust, resulting in a poor transition into high school.

Your comment in *Boy Smarts Action Study Guide* about turnaround teachers and "the amazing power that teachers have to tip the scale for boys from risk to resilience" grabbed my attention. After reading your books, I believe that Michael has a visual-hand's-on learning style that has not been fully understood or appreciated. Still, I know that Michael, who carries a chip on his shoulder, can be hard to teach, as I too struggle with him at home. He talks back and has a hard time accepting help.

I would appreciate your thoughts about how his Grade 7 teachers can help him be more successful. Does school success really boil down to the *chemistry* between student and teacher? What do turnaround teachers do when they encounter a student like my son—stubborn, argumentative, and resistant to writing?

Dorothy

Dear Dorothy,

After more than two dozen years of responding to parental concerns about boys' underachievement and considerable time supporting teachers to take caring and constructive action, I agree with the school principal to a point. I believe that one person's influence can help nudge boys from being at-risk to becoming resilient and successful learners. However, I also believe that while good relational *chemistry* may sound a bit mystical, there are teaching practices and approaches to students that can help struggling boys find their way.

If we are to help kids become adaptable and strengthen their ingenuity, we need to respond to their unique ways of learning and tap into our own adaptive abilities.

Many boys who dislike conventional school learning—and find writing boring—often delight in playing with ideas visually—with *Lego*, puzzles and computer games, for example. These boys may be fascinated with a project blueprint, concentrating on its image at great length, as absorbed as others might be by a captivating novel.

I recall how years ago I worked with one 11 year old boy who, like your son, also resisted written assignments. While he refused learning assistance for his writing weaknesses, I backed off from expectations about his writing and emphasized instead his visual strengths as an illustrator, working meanwhile to develop insight into his learning style and internal motivation.

One day late in September, he voluntarily showed up for his first visit to the editor's table at the back of the classroom, quietly pointing to a drawing at the top of his page. While I could not help but notice his sketchy writing below the drawing, I focussed on his editing request by probing further: "What kind of input about your drawing are you looking for?" He hesitated. "Do you like it?" he asked shyly. I did indeed, but, sensing his uneasiness, I was careful to not gush or smother him with too much praise. He smiled and left the table.

As Aaron's comfort and courage to seek feedback grew, I was cautiously optimistic that we were on to something good. He returned to the editing table several times over the following weeks and we discussed aspects of illustrating that he had questions about. He was integrating ideas from our class discussions, not through writing, but through creating illustrations of these ideas. The librarian helped by locating a couple of instructional drawing books that he eagerly devoured. Both the librarian and I noted that as his comfort with drawing increased, so did his participation in classroom activities and discussions. Sometimes I had to prompt him to elaborate on the meaning of his illustrations, but each time it became clear that he understood the concepts we were learning. It seemed that once Aaron created a mental picture of an idea and could SEE how it fit with what he already knew learning became much easier for him, and intrinsically motivating. Like many visual-spatial thinkers, Aaron seemed to grasp ideas intuitively, almost instantly, without really understanding all aspects of the idea, sometimes even missing steps in logic.

I'll not forget the first time he invited me to comment on his Halloween storyboard which contained a surprising amount of written expression. "What would you like me to comment on today?" His response surprised me. "Dots," he said. We briefly discussed the role punctuation had in written expression and how dots—periods—had a special job to let the reader know that the idea the sentence conveyed was complete. In this moment I recognized that while I needed to increase expectations to correspond with Aaron's development, I also saw clearly how his previous classroom difficulties were magnified when he felt pressured to write words down. I came to more fully understand that when Aaron was not expressing ideas visually, he was not thinking optimally.

As Aaron became a regular at the editing table, his newfound interest in written expression grew. By February he became a weekly contributor of cartoon drawings—which included narrative writing—to the principal's newsletter. The principal wisely published Aaron's creative efforts and even sought his input to design a cartoon poster for a bicycle safety contest he was planning for.

Although Aaron's writing ability lagged behind that of his peers that year, his enthusiasm for learning gradually took off. I lost track of him until several years later.

As I was leaving a bank, and was stopped by Aaron, now a young man, he asked: "You knew I was smart, didn't you?" he said. I smiled knowingly, and we briefly talked about his step-by-step growing school success and his present career aspirations as a graphic artist.

Aaron's growing resilience was more complicated than a single-step *bounce back* from adversity. Turnaround experiences don't always happen with a single event or even within a single school year. Transformative experiences can be partial or interrupted, roundabout and unpredictable. Constructive experiences in earlier years can provide boys with a baseline for positive memories and a familiarity with success that they can return to in their imagination, during and beyond the challenging years of high school.

Wise teachers recognize that students will not succeed if day after day they are asked to engage in activities that do not reflect their unique ways of learning.

To help you work with your son's teachers to facilitate positive and even turnaround learning experiences, I offer the following suggestions based on best teaching practices.

Put Relationships First

Some students who drag their feet into the classroom, or skip out to the halls at the first opportunity, often become labelled as unteachable. These students can spiral downward into despair, believing they are on their own. Yet most of us know that kids don't care how much we know until they know how much we care. Teachers activate resilience when they convey empathic support, validation of their students' feelings, and respect for their students' struggles. Teachers who wisely separate student learning outcomes and achievement from the students themselves may become compassionately curious. What makes this person, here and now, shut down? What makes him or her light up? These teachers recognize that discouraged students are often doing the best they can at any given time, given their skill and stress levels.

Believe That All Students Can Achieve Their Learning Potential

Transformative teachers and parents seek to reframe a student's struggle from being at-risk to being at-promise. They believe that everyone has the power to learn and grow. They learn how to recast problems as learning opportunities. Knowing that others' belief becomes internalized, these teachers have faith that current struggles are temporary, and may even be necessary parts of a still unknown big picture.

To listen to a 10 year old boy himself offer a brief but powerful keynote speech about believing in students to 20,000 teachers as they prepare for the upcoming school year, visit the **YouTube** website and search for Dalton Sherman's *"Do you believe in me?"*.

Seek What's Beneath a Struggle With Learning

Recognize that beneath their bravado or veneer of indifference, boys have many worries. They worry about performing well enough socially, academically, athletically, and in other arenas. They worry whether they are manly enough. Ultimately they worry about not fitting in. When boys are resistant or disengaged at school, teachers advance resiliency by considering how boys are often attempting to manage their anxiety and frustration in unskilled ways.

Given that a boy's school achievement and behaviour most likely represent his version of adapting to his life circumstances to ensure his survival, successful teachers do not write off boys as unteachable, but tune into his version of reality, seeking a deeper understanding of a boy's struggle. These thoughtful teachers do not grab at a simple set of pre-determined explanations such as power-seeking or attention-seeking but consider multiple and unique explanations. They do not distance themselves from boys through alienating labels and diagnoses, but are receptive to learning what they can about a particular boy, in a particular place, at a particular time.

Provide Flexible Learning Environments

Rather than expect students to mould themselves to the curriculum, transformative teachers adjust the curriculum and learning activities to meet varied learning needs. They build when they can on students' strengths. When students are off task, transformative teachers ask, "What's the task?" recognizing that students need multiple options for taking in information; for making sense of ideas; and for expressing their knowledge.

A recent 2009 British Columbia document, *A Guide to Adaptations and Modifications*, offers a starting point for differentiating instruction and creating flexible learning options for all students:

- alternatives to written assignments to demonstrate knowledge and understanding

- audio tapes, electronic texts, or a peer helper to assist with assigned readings

- access to a computer for written assignments (e.g. use of word prediction software, spellchecker, idea generator)

- advance organizers/graphic organizers to assist with following classroom presentations

- extended time to complete assignments or tests

- support to develop and practise study skills; for example, in a learning assistance block

- use of computer software that provides text to speech/speech to text capabilities

- pre-teaching key vocabulary or concepts; multiple exposure to materials

Set Realistic Expectations That Are Rigorous But Reachable

When boys are floundering at school, teachers can help them to see what's possible by holding a deep belief in their innate competence and self-righting capacities, and by challenging boys to perform at a level beyond what they believe they can do. Yet they are careful not to set the bar too high. At the same time that transformative teachers know that high expectations produce good results, and low expectations produce poor ones, they also understand that out-of-reach expectations may hinder fledging growth. By ensuring a sensible congruence between expectation and capability, teachers can set the bar just high enough to be a realistic challenge. Over time, sometimes months, sometimes even years, students can develop realistic hope and optimism. They can shift from aching, helpless self-talk of a victim such as, "Nothing works, no matter what I do" or "I'm not smart enough," and begin to hear the quiet inner voice of encouragement: "Even though this is tough, I have what it takes to figure it out." Transformative teachers teach students rather than standards. They learn to return, over and over, to their own inner voices of wisdom, responding in creative ways to their deep desire to help each student, of whatever stripe, to learn and thrive.

Maintain Perspective With Mistakes

Capabilities for resilience are often linked to a student's response to mistakes and failure, not to the mistakes themselves. Teachers who facilitate transformative learning experiences find ways to convey that dwelling on mistakes blocks resilience, and that blunders are simply part of the learning process. Caring adults help boys understand that mistakes are not the problem, but a necessary part of learning. The problem is the fear of making mistakes and being humiliated. Caring adults can help normalize mistakes by revealing their own slip-ups in an appropriate way, and demonstrating that trying again, and sometimes again and again, takes courage and self-acceptance.

Provide Frequent, Timely Feedback

Observing boys play video games has taught me that boys appreciate frequent feedback about their learning. Turnaround teachers likely know that when feedback is timely, student-involved, targeted, and specific to the content being learned, boys feel empowered. Through close observation of boys in the process of learning, regular collection of feedback on their learning, and the design of modest classroom experiments, teachers can learn much about how boys learn and, more specifically, how they respond to particular teaching approaches. From these observations classroom assessment can be designed which provide useful feedback on what, how much, and how well boys are learning. Teachers can then use this information to refocus their teaching to help boys make their learning more satisfying and successful.

Mentor With Sensitivity

Understanding that students have not yet fully developed their full capacity for rational decision-making, caring teachers are more likely to take the time to understand boys' unique personalities and temperaments. Some sensitive teachers may help students who are engaged in destructive thought patterns to gain some perspective, perhaps even introducing simple experiments encouraging an optimistic kind of self-talk.

Because many boys' process thought and feelings through action, transformative teachers respond creatively to these boys' fidgeting and jolts of energy in ways that help boys feel at ease. When they are discussing a potentially fraught situation with a boy, they do not corner a boy, but they may walk, engage in minor activity, and talk intermittently. When boys are silent and *turtle-like*, turnaround teachers give space. They respect boys' silence, knowing that talking too much and moving too close can be experienced as intrusive, as trying too hard, even as not being real. They also respect differing needs for eye contact, knowing that many boys feel crowded by an eyeball-to-eyeball stare. Mostly, caring adults lead by example. When they inadvertently offend a boy, caring adults find a sensitive and respectful way to express their regret, knowing that a simple apology does not translate into loss of status.

Sidestep Conflict

Transformative teachers welcome differing personalities among students. Knowing that some boys are just more easily triggered than others, they can often diffuse potential conflict, or challenges to their authority, with a light touch. Insisting on doing things his own way can be the boy's method of showing he is his own boss, which can be productive for him on one level. It can also be a way of avoiding his anxiety. Eye-rolling, muttering, and smiling at inopportune moments are meant to provoke adults and also to save face. When adults insist that students do things their way, they risk raising the stakes in a new, heightened level of confrontation. To build resiliency perceptive teachers stay outside of a boy's conflict cycle. When an adolescent boy says, "This homework sucks," resilience-building teachers do not get drafted into a power struggle. They may even express genuine curiosity: "Maybe if we talk about what you don't like, we might be able to find a solution that we can both be happy about." When a boy digs in his heels, wise teachers refrain from getting hooked in. They don't fight, they don't cave in. They seek a negotiated solution that satisfies everyone.

Use Restorative Discipline That Promotes Self-Discipline

Accepting boys for who they are and not who we want them to be does not mean we allow a free-for-all. However, we recognize that the unflinching enforcement of rules does not create inner responsibility or self-discipline.

When boys act out, transformative teachers know well that boys learn respect for self and others when they experience respect first-hand. Turnaround teachers commonly attribute the best possible motive to behaviour, knowing that rebellious and antisocial behaviours are probably flawed strategies of adaptation that worked for some reason at some point, but have become maladaptive.

Resiliency-building teachers know that unrealistic behavioural contracts or school suspensions reduce a boy's sense of connectedness to school, leaving him with less and less to lose. Besides, today's macho peer culture typically offers false rewards to boys who buck the system, as witnessed when peers give a hero's welcome after a suspension or when a contract is broken. Creative and sensitive educators find strategies of restorative discipline that fit the student and the situation, that teach rather than punish, and that provide opportunities for positive transformation.

Maximize Student Involvement

Authentic learning experiences provide opportunities for students to make real and meaningful decisions about their school lives, increasing intrinsic motivation and commitment to action. When we realize that student motivation is driven by a great variety of needs such as belonging, autonomy, challenge, mastery, and fun, we begin to grasp the underlying causes of discouragement as we work with boys to design and negotiate solutions.

Activate Student, Peer and Community Involvement

Student, peer, and community input and partnerships help boys to overcome adversity. By establishing an advocacy club to help boys and others focus on a boy's strengths, interests, and goals, transformative teachers use the power of communities—especially cross-age and peer mentoring—to further boys' success.

These teachers are alert to creating opportunities for empowering youth in ways such as the following:

- restorative justice circles to engage youth to develop ethics and concern for others

- student input to create assignments, make rules, and come to decisions about matters that affect youth

- regular class meetings that address teacher and student needs and concerns

Involve Parents

When boys are striking out, parents need to be consulted as authentic partners. Parents and teachers may look at children's learning from different perspectives, but they share a common goal—making sure that children receive the best education possible. Students benefit when parents and teachers communicate in an atmosphere of mutual respect, and work together for success.

Facilitate Respectful Assessment or Planning Meetings

When an assessment meeting of a boy's learning support team takes place, effective teachers take a thoughtful look at their school's practice for reporting psychometric assessment results—or any results for that matter—to parents, students, and others. They ensure that the meeting is structured so that the discussion, while acknowledging the testing results, also includes a holistic view of the boy that emphasizes his capabilities.

They ensure that the boy is not objectified, but invited to give input in a manner that isn't perfunctory or coercive. Transformative teachers create real opportunities for boys to offer alternative suggestions. Most importantly, transformative teachers ensure that assessment information is presented respectfully so that the meeting is not a masquerade of power, and neither the boy nor his parents are shamed.

Seek Authentic Solutions

When boys feel backed into a corner with a so-called choice such as whether or not to sign a behaviour contract, progress can be hindered and even stalled. Youth are alert to the manipulations that adults sometimes use to induce compliance. Boys may sign the contract to end the intervention meeting, but typically have no intention of following through. Effective teachers balance their own adult desires to get boys to make the *right* choices with the boy's desire to have his needs recognized and listened to. These teachers know well that less can be more, and prefer smaller, realistic steps that lead to practical action over large-scale schemes of conversion. A stern tightening of the screws may chasten a few boys, and may even drive them, in the short run, to bring up their grades. However, grades do not help intrinsic motivation. We need strategies that address not only short-term goals, but also long-range ones—such as the development of talents, strengths, and the lifelong love of learning.

When we are truly focussed on what's in a child's best interest over the long term, when we are willing to question conventional wisdom, we may, at times, find our own resilience depleted. We may worry that our child is taxing the system, that a particular teacher has derailed our child, or that the system itself is deaf and dumb. Yet I know from experience that blaming outside forces, or trying to go it alone, leads to bitterness and defeat. As we work toward the development of compassion toward young people, we help them best as we minister to ourselves with kindness, compassion, and an awareness that all adversity is temporary. We can treasure small victories, tiny transformations that may, with time and patience and nurturance, grow into major ones.

Collaborating to Generate Positive Solutions
• • • • • • • • •

"It's not that I'm so smart, it's just that I stay with problems longer."

Albert Einstein

THIS is a challenging time for boys, and for those who mentor boys. Once teachers might have said to students, "If you'll pay close attention to what I teach you, you'll learn what you need to know." Today, we are acutely aware that we don't know all the answers that children will need, or even the questions they will struggle with.

Parents are alarmed by national statistics that point to boys' lagging school achievement. They also worry about problems at home—how to keep boys on task, why boys are playing video games rather than reading, why they are lollygagging instead of completing chores, and why they seem so disengaged at times. Ironically, some parents also worry about girls who, while they may have earned higher grades than boys at school, may be constrained more than ever by the cultural dictates of beauty and femininity. With the recent *Maclean's* headline shrieking, ***Outraged Moms, Trashy Daughters: How Did Feminism Come to This*** (August 2010), it is clear that the gender struggle is not limited to boys' lagging achievement. Worries about gender and culture now seem bundled with larger parenting challenges—how to balance the inculcation of discipline with self-esteem, for example, or how to protect children from the deluge of sex and violence in the media.

In the face of such worries, it may be tempting to grab hold of any solution—perhaps a pill that will help boys sit still longer, or single-gender classrooms.

However, we have learned that our approaches must be nuanced, respectful of individual differences. We know that while subtle differences in brain design may account for some different tendencies in boys and girls, we also know that there can be wide variations throughout the gender matrix, and that environment and culture are strong influences. We also recognize that the individual temperament matters, and that different learning styles call for different approaches: perhaps more opportunity to engage in interpersonal relationship, more visual-spatial learning, or more active learning and movement.

I do not stand alone in my advocacy of different learning designs for different students with different learning needs. Over the past decade best-practice teacher research has stressed that teachers steer clear of traditional stand and deliver methods of instruction. We need to move away from what recent data from the **National Institute of Child Health and Human Development Early Child Care Research Network** (2005) reveals as the primary focus in schools—the finding that most school instructional time is composed of seatwork and whole-class instruction led by the teacher. In order to engage boys and the wider community, we must move more and more toward education that emphasizes collaboration and relevant problem-solving.

As advances in technology and communication keep accelerating, we may question whether schools were even designed to teach the kinds of students we have now. Certainly discussions with boys at school, in the community, and in my office have revealed that boys' perceptions and expectations of schooling are different than the ones which boys held years ago. Boys who grow up in the new digital world, sometimes called digital natives, think and process information fundamentally differently than those of us who are digital immigrants, and these differences run deep.

We must learn to take advantage of the wireless technology that boys are using and learning from. Our dazzling digital landscape is not the cause of boys' disengagement; instead it is a wonderful opportunity for parents and teachers to rethink their ideas about learning and knowledge.

Yes, boys need less screen time, less medication, less punitive control and more opportunities to create, explore, and care for others. They also need learning experiences that prepare them to be productive and creative thinkers who can thrive in a world of constant change.

To strengthen our approach we might lean on the wisdom of Albert Einstein, and be willing to "stay with problems longer". We might become more comfortable taking the time to linger with questions.

It will be by working together that we will find the varied and imaginative solutions that will help boys grow into men of courage and compassion.

So What Can We Do?

Throughout this book, I've offered concrete suggestions for helping boys to read and develop a love of literacy, to expand their emotional world, and to cultivate and practice their leadership, nurturing, and organizational skills. My intention is to stimulate discussion and action, especially between home and school.

More than any other group in our society, it is parents who care about making schools, classrooms, and learning work for their boys. When boys are striking out, it is essential that parents be consulted as partners. Parents and teachers may have different perspectives on boys' learning, but they share a common goal—making sure that children receive the best education possible. Mutually respectful communication between home and school takes advantage of both perspectives to provide children with the kind of care and education that will help them thrive.

Clearly, we need a holistic approach that does not pit educators and parents against each other—or others in the community—but maintains a clear focus on finding positive plans of action.

To encourage thoughtful and balanced discussion about boys' differing needs, I published the *Boy Smarts Action Study Guide* to accompany my first book about boys, *Boy Smarts: Mentoring Boys for Success at School*, inviting readers to think critically and imaginatively about ways to help struggling boys.

Because a one-size-fits-all approach simply will not work, the guide offers hundreds of questions or talking points that consider a broad range issues that lead to positive and productive action. The guide provides the following key ideas to help *kick-start* thoughtful conversations about boys:

1. Many students struggle with learning, but the learning problems of boys have become increasingly hard to ignore.

2. Efforts to raise the achievement of boys must be made without threatening the gains made by girls.

3. We need to avoid over–generalizing about causal links between gender and achievement.

4. As boys are not a homogeneous group, the use of statistics about boys as a group can at times be limiting or misleading.

5. Since it has been noted that there is more overlap between the achievment of boys and girls than difference, we need to be careful not to exaggerate small discrepancies in academic assessments.

6. Brain differences should be understood as relative tendencies only.

7. Gender becomes part of the process of differentiation. Some boys and girls may learn differently.

8. Boys' academic underachievement should be considered in its social context.

9. Just as there is no single cause of the underachievement of boys, there is no single solution.

10. Each school community needs to consider gender and achievement in its own context and tailor strategies that fit their circumstances.

11. To teach boys effectively, we need to understand and appreciate boys' gifts and talents.

12. Effective parents and teachers focus on finding solutions rather than accentuating the problems.

With these key ideas as a starting point, a small group of concerned parents and teachers can address their concerns about boys' education in a positive and strategic manner.

As we work together, we can raise expectations for boys as we once did for girls, but this time we will be more mindful not to pit the needs of one group against the needs of another. We can honour each child's powerful desire to learn, and ensure that everything we do as parents and teachers will keep this powerful desire alive. We can help boys tap into their strengths while we also create language-rich learning environments as well as the physical play, hands-on and real-life learning I have encouraged here.

At home parents will also help by ensuring their boys are immersed in language from an early age: singing, talking, and reading frequently to young boys; taking them to the library as well as sitting with them as they play video games; organizing time for them to become quiet and reflective while also providing opportunities for them to be as active as they need to be; and fostering their love of outdoor education, music, fine arts, and the art of conversation.

At school we can work together to ensure that boys are presented with realistic and achievable goals that reflect their differing motivations and aptitudes. We can ensure that learning activities are relevant, provide frequent breaks, and create classrooms that capitalize on technological resources. We can teach boys to become creative thinkers—open to new learning, able to tackle still unknown questions with competence and imagination.

If we work together with faith that children will find their way, they will.

We can celebrate the uniqueness of each child, male and female, securely attached to relationship.

With our support, empathy, and creative vision, children who struggle will find an inner core of strength that allows them to be comfortable in who they are; a resilience that allows them to meet new challenges with optimism; and a deep respect for self, family members, and others in the wider community.

Barry MacDonald is an educator and *Registered Clinical Counsellor* who is a champion for strong families, strong schools, and an advocate for boys. A sought-after speaker and authority on boys and learning, he has worked with parents, educators, and youth for over twenty-five years, nationally and internationally.

Barry's ideas have been presented on radio, television, and in numerous print media. He was also identified as one of ***25 Influential People to Watch*** by the **Vancouver Sun** in 2005 for his innovative approaches to mentoring boys for success at school and life.

Barry's message about helping boys recently struck just the right chord with school leaders, including Dr. Avis Glaze, a woman of influence who has served as ***Ontario's Secretariat for Literacy and Numeracy*** and received ***The Order of Ontario***; she is widely known for her innovative professional development initiatives aimed toward improving achievement for all students. Dr. Glaze remarked:

"Barry MacDonald's compelling presentation is one of the best I have ever seen. His keynote address at the ***National Principals' Conference*** was balanced, insightful and presented with perspicacity. He offers a framework and an array of strategies that will indeed make a tremendous difference in the lives of boys struggling at school. Barry is an outstanding speaker who wisely knows the place of attunement and humour, and indeed should be heard by every educator and parent."

✸ ✸ ✸ ✸ ✸ ✸ ✸ ✸

Visit Barry MacDonald's website: ***www.MentoringBoys.com***